NEW DIRECTIONS FOR HIGHER EDUCATION

Martin Kramer, *University of California, Berkeley*
EDITOR-IN-CHIEF

Recognizing Faculty Work: Reward Systems for the Year 2000

Robert M. Diamond
Syracuse University

Bronwyn E. Adam
Syracuse University

EDITORS

Number 81, Spring 1993

JOSSEY-BASS PUBLISHERS
San Francisco

RECOGNIZING FACULTY WORK: REWARD SYSTEMS FOR THE YEAR 2000
Robert M. Diamond, Bronwyn E. Adam (eds.)
New Directions for Higher Education, no. 81
Martin Kramer, Editor-in-Chief

Microfilm copies of issues and articles are available in 16mm and 35mm, as well as microfiche in 105mm, through University Microfilms Inc., 300 North Zeeb Road, Ann Arbor, Michigan 48106.

LC 85-644752   ISSN 0271-0560   ISBN 1-55542-691-3

NEW DIRECTIONS FOR HIGHER EDUCATION is part of The Jossey-Bass Higher and Adult Education Series and is published quarterly by Jossey-Bass Inc., Publishers, 350 Sansome Street, San Francisco, California 94104-1310 (publication number USPS 990-880). Second-class postage paid at San Francisco, California, and at additional mailing offices. POSTMASTER: Send address changes to New Directions for Higher Education, Jossey-Bass Inc., Publishers, 350 Sansome Street, San Francisco, California 94104-1310.

SUBSCRIPTIONS for 1993 cost $45.00 for individuals and $60.00 for institutions, agencies, and libraries.

EDITORIAL CORRESPONDENCE should be sent to the Editor-in-Chief, Martin Kramer, 2807 Shasta Road, Berkeley, California 94708.

Cover photograph and random dot by Richard Blair/Color & Light © 1990.

The paper used in this journal is acid-free and meets the strictest guidelines in the United States for recycled paper (50 percent recycled waste, including 10 percent postconsumer waste). Manufactured in the United States of America.

10% POST
CONSUMER
WASTE

CONTENTS

Editors' Notes

It is not an easy time for higher education in the United States. Major reports from the National Endowment for the Humanities, the National Institute of Education, the Association of American Colleges, and the Carnegie Foundation for the Advancement of Teaching have called for greater emphasis on teaching, clearer statements of institutional missions, improved assessment practices, and the development of cohesive and appropriate curricula.

In the popular press, a number of authors have made their reputations by decrying the state of higher education, often employing unrepresentative or distorted data or examples. At the same time, politicians have expediently focused a critical eye on colleges and universities, which they assert are poor in quality and wasteful of resources. Meanwhile, the public—in particular, recruiters and business employers—claim that many college graduates cannot write effectively or speak convincingly and are unprepared for positions that require computer, computational, interpersonal, and problem-solving skills. While critics have tended to overlook the many positive examples of quality programs, strong teaching, and significant research in our colleges and universities, we do have problems in higher education that need to be addressed. In an era of unprecedented social and political change, structures and systems in higher education must be reevaluated in light of larger changes in the culture and world around the academy.

Conflicting Priorities

Institutional change is never easy; however, in the present context, the process has been complicated by major budget cuts and simultaneous demands for quick action. This combination can be lethal. In some state systems, budgets are being reduced at the same time that institutions are being asked to accept more students and to revise curricula or teaching methods to serve more diverse student populations. Faculty feel pressure from all segments of the education community—from administrators and department heads who need more of their time for a host of activities related to teaching, service, and research to students who, as consumers, want greater access to their teachers. Faculty face continued commitments to scholarship and published research, and many faculty understandably spend considerable time on these activities to ensure promotion, tenure, and annual merit pay increases.

Unfortunately, the reality of conflicting demands and priorities has been reduced by some to a tired debate, pitting teaching as an academic pursuit against scholarly research endeavors. Such dichotomous thinking is self-defeating and denies the integral nature of academic life. Research and teaching are best viewed as interrelated efforts that college and university professors pursue sometimes in equal measure and simultaneously and at other times in intermittent fashion, but always as interrelated activities. In order to properly recognize and reward faculty work, we must reconsider the role of the professoriate and develop promotion, tenure, and merit reward systems that are appropriate for individual faculty members and consonant with the priorities of the institution and the values of the individual disciplines.

Recognizing Faculty Work

Initiatives are under way across the country to rethink the nature of scholarship, to redefine faculty work, and to redesign the reward systems used to recognize professional effort and achievement. The focus of this volume, *Recognizing Faculty Work: Reward Systems for the Year 2000,* is the reconceptualization of the extrinsic and intrinsic reward systems operating in higher education. This revision must take into full consideration the needs of the larger community, the priorities of higher education institutions, the interests of faculty, and the education goals of students.

The central objective here is to give practical assistance to those engaged in the review of their faculty reward systems. Each chapter has been designed to address major issues relating to promotion, tenure, and merit pay and, at the same time, outline practical models for change that have been developed by institutions engaged in the process of clarifying their institutional missions and modifying their faculty reward structures.

In Chapter One, Robert M. Diamond focuses on the faculty reward system in general. And, in Chapter Two, in setting the stage for the chapters that follow and describing the characteristics of an effective reward structure, he proposes a model for change, discusses the important role of the central administration in establishing a climate for change, and describes issues that can emerge during the change process.

In Chapter Three, Bronwyn E. Adam and Alton O. Roberts describe a number of different approaches to redefining faculty work, emphasizing the need for multiple, context-specific definitions. Statements from a number of disciplines articulating what faculty do in their academic fields are included. These redefinitions differ in approach and structure but provide a working base on which academic departments can develop their own criteria for rewarding faculty work. This chapter can also sensitize those who serve on cross-disciplinary promotion and tenure committees to the necessity of honoring the differences among the disciplines.

In Chapter Four, Alton O. Roberts, Jon F. Wergin, and Bronwyn E. Adam present sample documents from four institutions that illustrate different ways of changing institutional priorities and reward systems to recognize a broader range of faculty work. A report on a collaborative venture among seven campuses is also included. Finally, an additional ten institutions and their initiatives are highlighted. These practical reports provide insights into the variety of issues that can emerge during this change process as well as guidance for initiating change on individual campuses.

Promotion, tenure, and merit pay are but three of the reasons why faculty do what they do. In Chapter Five, Robert C. Froh, Robert J. Menges, and Charles J. Walker focus on faculty activities that are pursued for reasons other than formal extrinsic rewards, and they describe how consideration of intrinsic motivation factors can help an institution recognize and take into account all of the factors that influence faculty work.

Finally, in Chapter Six, Robert C. Froh, Peter J. Gray, and Leo M. Lambert examine ways in which the broad range of work of an individual faculty member might be presented in a professional portfolio. They emphasize the evaluation of teaching, scholarly and creative work, and service and suggest various means of collecting, organizing, and presenting documentation.

The Appendix, "Departmental Statements on Faculty Rewards," focuses on academic unit–based faculty reward structures. Two examples illustrate how distinctly different departments at the same institution describe their missions and guidelines for faculty rewards.

In order for institutional change to be successful, those directing the process must have a plan that develops ownership in the final system by everyone who will be involved in or affected by its implementation. It is our hope that this volume will facilitate that process.

In closing, we thank our colleagues, at Syracuse University and elsewhere, who have been instrumental in this initiative to reconsider faculty roles and rewards. Chief among them are Russell Edgerton of the American Association of Higher Education and the fine staff at the Center for Instructional Development. We also thank Ralph Lundgren of the Lilly Endowment and Preston Forbes of the Fund for the Improvement of Postsecondary Education, who have through their programs encouraged and supported this initiative.

Robert M. Diamond
Bronwyn E. Adam
Editors

ROBERT M. DIAMOND *is assistant vice chancellor for instructional development and professor of instructional development, design, and evaluation at Syracuse University. He also is director of* Changing Priorities in Higher Education, *a project sponsored by the Lilly Endowment.*

BRONWYN E. ADAM *is assistant project director at the Center for Instructional Development, Syracuse University.*

*Institutional change is a challenging task best undertaken
systematically and thoughtfully, with respect for individual
differences and the complexity of the worlds within and
surrounding the academy.*

Changing Priorities and the Faculty Reward System

Robert M. Diamond

No process in higher education receives more attention, generates more debate on individual campuses among faculty and administrators, or creates more frustration than the promotion and tenure system. For new faculty facing the rigors of the tenure system, the institutional reward structure determines priorities and focuses young professors' energies for the first six or seven years of their academic careers. For faculty serving on promotion and tenure committees, the system entails months of meetings, endless debates, and often uncomfortable decisions. For administrators who must make final determinations based on the recommendations of committees, deans, chairs, and department faculty—recommendations that are not necessarily consonant—the current faculty recognition and reward system often presents problems of conflicting priorities and no-win decisions.

Many of the problems associated with the promotion and tenure system are inherent to any decision-making process; others are idiosyncratic to the concept and role of tenure. Originally established as a means of protecting the rights of faculty to express their opinions openly and without fear of reprisals by administrators, the tenure system has come to be equated with job security in the minds of most faculty, particularly during this period of declining enrollments and a faltering economy. As the job market in higher education has tightened, institutions have attempted to "cap" the size of their faculties through normal attrition and by limiting the number of younger faculty who receive tenure. Institutional budget cuts have further increased pressures to tighten standards for tenure. At the same time, there is growing concern over the criteria used in the tenure process, criteria that have carried over to the promotion and merit pay areas as well.

These criteria, which in large part determine faculty activities, have increasingly defined faculty productivity in terms of research and publication. As a result, students complain about poor teaching and misdirected priorities, and institutions are told that they have lost touch with their central mission of teaching students and serving their communities. If the American higher education system is to succeed as an enterprise, the faculty reward system on each campus must be compatible with the institution's central mission. Otherwise, faculty energies and talents will be wasted, and our colleges and universities will be centers of increasing tension and frustration.

The institutional reward system must send a clear signal to faculty that what is valued by the institution will be rewarded at all points in the promotion and tenure system. As Marchese (1992, p. 4) has noted, many of the problems that we face in higher education are systemic: "The problems that exist are far less those of individual behaviors than they are of the system. It is the system that dictates what faculty do, and that deflates morale. From the trenches, it's a system of contradictory messages from above, of perverse funding patterns, out-of-kilter expectations and rewards, archaic personnel practices, of penury in support of innovation; it's a system that demands more as it gives less and frustrates best intentions time after time. From the trenches, and to my eyes, the critics blame the victim." Faculty and administration can and should work together to reform their personnel practices, from teacher training through appointment, promotion, tenure, and merit pay decisions.

Role of the Faculty Reward System in Establishing Priorities

If, given competing demands, the problems of the institution and the needs of the student are not the top priorities of faculty, what are the dynamics at work in the system? Many observers argue that the present criteria for rewarding faculty work are based on the scientific model of research and publication and are counterproductive to reaching larger academic goals. Boyer (1987) reported that divided loyalties and competing career concerns appeared with regularity and seemed consistently to sap the vitality of the baccalaureate experience. In his follow-up publication, *Scholarship Reconsidered: Priorities for the Professoriate,* Boyer (1990, pp. 15–16) argued that "a wide gap now exists between the myth and the reality of academic life. Almost all colleges pay lip service to the trilogy of teaching, research, and service, but when it comes to making judgments about professional performance, the three rarely are assigned equal merit. . . . The time has come to move beyond the tired old 'teaching versus research' debate and give the familiar and honorable term 'scholarship' a broader, more capacious meaning, one that brings legitimacy to the full scope of academic work."

Boyer's position seems to be shared by many in academe. A recent study of responses from over twenty-three thousand faculty, chairs, deans, and administrators at research universities indicated that even those most directly involved with the present reward system feel that the balance between research and teaching is inappropriate and needs to be modified (Gray, Froh, and Diamond, 1992). As one young faculty member lamented, "As a new junior professor, I have come into the profession with a strong interest in research but an equally strong interest in serving students by helping them learn both in and outside of the classroom. The attitude I'm receiving from all levels . . . is that research is what counts. If the other areas of service and teaching are lacking but research is strong, then promotions will follow. Unfortunately I think this is the wrong message to be sending faculty" (Gray, Froh, and Diamond, 1992, p. 13).

Most significant, the results of this study indicate that an effort to modify the promotion and tenure system to recognize and reward strong teaching would be supported by the majority of faculty, chairs, deans, and central administrators on the forty-seven campuses surveyed. Data from a study of over fifteen hundred faculty members from institutions through-out the state of Virginia also strongly support the approach of giving more weight to "vigorously evaluated teaching" and developing a promotion and tenure system that balances teaching and research differentially for different faculty members (Survey Research Laboratory, 1991).

Work has begun at the level of the academic disciplines to reconsider definitions of scholarly, creative, and intellectual contributions. The reports of professional associations that articulate the broad range of activities in which their faculties engage reveal one common theme across disciplines: Important faculty work is not being rewarded. Service, teaching, and creativity are risky priorities for faculty members seeking promotion or tenure at many institutions. A draft report from the American Historical Association Ad Hoc Committee on Redefining Scholarly Work (1992, p. 1) reflects this concern: "This debate over priorities is not discipline-specific but extends across the higher education community. Nevertheless, each discipline has specific concerns and problems. For history, the privilege given to the monograph in promotion and tenure has led to the undervaluing of other activities central to the life of the discipline—writing textbooks, developing courses and curricula, documentary editing, museum exhibitions, and film projects to name but a few."

The same problem appears in drama departments with the production of plays, in English or writing departments when faculty members work in the local communities to develop literacy programs, and in management, economics, sociology, and retailing when professors' skills are used to help community groups address significant problems. Stated bluntly, the focus on research and publication and the mad dash for federal funds and external grants has diverted energies away from important faculty work and has had a direct and negative impact on the quality of classroom instruction and the ability of institutions to provide support to and involve their communities. Energies have also been diverted from types of research that do not fall within the traditional publication realm. Real limitations exist for faculty who want to ensure recognition for their scholarly pursuits. The choice is often between the types of research that intrigue and excite them and the types that can be represented in a publication and that appeal to the prestige journals and book publishers. The result has been a proliferation of what might be called "establishment research."

Characteristics of an Appropriate and Effective Promotion and Tenure System

In order for an institution to confront these issues in a proactive manner, the faculty reward structure must be modified so as to include a number of features rarely found in present promotion and tenure plans:

The system must be compatible with the mission statement of the institution. All colleges and universities are not alike. State institutions, private institutions, church-related colleges, urban and rural institutions all have their own agendas. There are institutions with a distinct research mission, while others are focused primarily on teaching and service. An effective promotion and tenure system must be sensitive to these differences and build on and support the mission statement of the institution. In order to support change in the reward system, the institutional mission statement must be realistic, operational, and sensitive to the unique characteristics and strengths of the institution. Such is not always the case. Many institutional mission statements are vaguely articulated, employing nonspecific language open to a variety of interpretations. Others express lofty ideals that are difficult to attain and impossible to assess. Recently, Samuel Hope, executive director of the National Office for Arts Accreditation in Higher Education, asserted, "From my perspective in accreditation, it is not unusual to see tremendous rhetorical emphasis on the mission-goal objectives equation within institutions and programs. It is also not unusual to see failure to work with the real meaning of this concept in various operational areas. The assessment of faculty work is one of these areas. . . . An institution cannot claim to have a unique mission . . . if it does not also have a unique approach to assessing the quality of faculty" (1992, p. 2).

The system must be sensitive to the differences among the disciplines. Several years ago, Syracuse University, with support from the Lilly Endowment and the Fund for the Improvement of Postsecondary Education, began a series of projects focused on the faculty reward system. As part of this initiative, a number of professional associations established task forces to develop statements articulating the range of activities that *could* be considered "scholarly" under a more inclusive definition of "scholarship." As this project has progressed, significant differences among the disciplines have become clear—differences in what faculty do across disciplines as well as in the language that they use to describe what they do. Reward systems must acknowledge and honor the inherent functional differences among the humanities, the social sciences, the sciences, and the professional schools. While some fields can easily accommodate the traditional terms of research, teaching, and service, others find the model developed by Eugene Rice more compatible. Rice (1991) has divided scholarly work into four components: (1) advancement of knowledge, which is, essentially, original research; (2) integration of knowledge, or synthesizing and reintegrating knowledge and revealing new patterns of meaning and new relationships between the parts and the whole; (3) application of knowledge, or professional practice directly related to an individual's scholarly specialization; and (4) transformation of knowledge through teaching, including pedagogical content knowledge and discipline-specific education theory.

For many of the disciplines, a review of the work of Rice, Boyer, and others has been an excellent place to begin. However, over time, some fields have chosen a model uniquely molded to the values and language of their disciplines. A single model or process is simply not realistic given the differences among the disciplines. Emerging from the professional associations are statements that scholars consider likely to facilitate generative dialogue in their fields. What we see evolving are standards and criteria that are functional at the institutional, college, and departmental levels and comprehensible to those outside the discipline who have key roles to play in the promotion and tenure process.

The system must be sensitive to the differences among individuals. We each bring to our work different strengths, interests, and perspectives. The establishment of an identical set of criteria for all faculty is unrealistic and can undermine the quality of an academic unit. The truth is that outstanding researchers are not necessarily great teachers, and great teachers are not always exceptional researchers. The goal for each department, school, or college should be to bring together talented individuals who can work together in a synergistic manner to reach the unit's goals. A department needs the great teacher who can motivate and excite entering students as much as it needs the quality researcher or author who can break new ground in the discipline and bring scholarly recognition to the department and institution. The reward system must also recognize that faculty, at different times in their careers, focus their attention in different areas. These shifts, in some cases, are the result of departmental assignments; in other cases, they are inherent to the disciplines involved. In some fields, faculty members' major research accomplishments are early in their careers; in others, a scholarly focus occurs later, when the individuals have had the opportunity to expand their perspectives.

The system must be sensitive to standards established by regional, state, and disciplinary accreditation associations. Various national accreditation groups have responded to the need for attention to teaching quality. Through a focus on learning outcomes, in consort with the broadening of definitions of faculty work by discipline-specific accreditation groups (discussed by Adam and Roberts, this volume), the assessment movement has not only provided guidelines for the development of evaluation criteria but at the same time actively supported the change process. Regional accreditation agencies have responded similarly. For example, in their most recent articulation of standards for accreditation, the Commission on Institutions of Higher Education, New England Association of Schools and Colleges (1992, pp. 13–18), included the following statement, which broadens the definition of scholarship and relates faculty work loads to institutional missions:

Scholarship and Research

All faculty pursue scholarship, an activity fundamental to the achievement of institutional purposes. Scholarship includes the ongoing application, utilization, and dissemination of existing knowledge as well as creative activity both within and outside the classroom. Scholarship and instruction are integrated and mutually supportive. Where compatible with the institution's purposes, research is undertaken. Research involves the creation, revision, or application of knowledge as undertaken by faculty and students. Physical and administrative resources together with academic services are adequate to support the institution's research commitment. Faculty workloads reflect the institution's research commitment. Policies and procedures related to research, including ethical considerations, are established and clearly communicated throughout the institution. The faculty play a substantive role in the development and administration of research policies and practices. Scholarship and research receive encouragement and support appropriate to the institution's purposes and objectives. Faculty and students are accorded the academic freedom to pursue scholarship and research.

Faculty

Faculty assignments and workloads are consistent with the institution's mission and purposes. They are equitably determined to allow faculty members adequate time to provide effective instruction, advise and evaluate students, continue professional growth, and participate in scholarship, research, and service compatible with the mission and purposes of the institution. Faculty workloads are reappraised periodically and adjusted as institutional conditions change. The faculty are demonstrably effective in carrying out their assigned responsibilities. The institution employs effective procedures for the regular evaluation of faculty appointments, performance, and retention. The evaluative criteria reflect the mission and purposes of the institution and the importance it attaches to the various responsibilities of faculty members, e.g., teaching, scholarship, creative activities, research, and professional and community service. The institution has equitable and broad based procedures for such evaluation, in which its expectations are stated clearly and weighted appropriately for use in the evaluative process.

Statements of this kind demonstrate that while accreditation agencies have often been considered unwelcome intruders into the daily operation of an institution, the proactive approach is a positive force in the current initiatives of colleges and universities to relate individual efforts to institutional priorities.

The system must develop an assessment program that is appropriate, perceived as fair, and workable. To reach this goal, a "selected professional portfolio," tailored around the specific responsibilities of an individual faculty member, is needed. This plan permits an in-depth evaluation of representative items and activities rather than the more customary quick review of often overlapping and redundant studies and publications. In disciplines in which it is appropriate, the professional portfolio can represent process as much as product. The portfolio plan provides an opportunity for faculty to represent their work so as to differentiate exceptional and innovative teaching, software and curriculum development, and significant research from the more commonplace activities that *all* faculty perform in their classrooms and laboratories.

Recently, Lynton (1992) discussed the need for documentation and the use of a "descriptive and reflective" essay within the selected professional portfolio. Such a dossier includes the usual products and "artifacts" such as published papers, books, reports, and course syllabi, as well as evaluations and letters of reference by students, clients, and external experts. But these items may not always be sufficient. As Lynton (1992, p. 30) observed, "If each scholarly activity is, in some sense, a voyage of exploration and discovery, it can be fully appreciated and evaluated only if one can follow the scholar on that journey." Hence the portfolio might also include a descriptive and reflective essay that provides the following: the specifics of the situation and the context for the activity; the objective of the activity; the choice of the specific content and methodology; the results of reflection-in-action in terms of unique and unexpected features encountered, adaptations made, inferences drawn, and lessons learned by the scholar; and the outcomes in terms of learning by the audience.

While the activities included in the various task force reports defining scholarly work vary across disciplines, the characteristics of these activities tend to be fairly consistent (see Adam and Roberts, this volume). The scholarly activities typically recognized in promotion and tenure structures share the following features:

- Require a high level of discipline-related expertise
- Break new ground or are innovative
- Can be replicated or elaborated
- Can be documented
- Can be peer-reviewed
- Have significance or impact

Attention to these features, in consort with criteria established by individual departments, can help us determine the scholarly nature of faculty work.

References

American Historical Association Ad Hoc Committee on Redefining Scholarly Work. *Redefining Historical Scholarship*. Washington, D.C.: American Historical Association, 1992.

Boyer, E. L. *College: The Undergraduate Experience in America*. New York: HarperCollins, 1987.

Boyer, E. L. *Scholarship Reconsidered: Priorities for the Professoriate*. Princeton, N.J.: Carnegie Foundation for the Advancement of Teaching, 1990.

Commission on Institutions of Higher Education, New England Association of Schools and Colleges, Inc. *Standards for Accreditation*. Winchester, Mass.: Commission on Institutions of Higher Education, New England Association of Schools and Colleges, Inc., 1992.

Gray, P. J., Froh, R. C., and Diamond, R. M. *A National Study of Research Universities on the Balance Between Research and Undergraduate Teaching*. Syracuse, N.Y.: Center for Instructional Development, Syracuse University, 1992.

Hope, S. "Assessing Faculty Work: Administrative Issues." Paper presented at the conference Redefinition and Assessment of Scholarship, Syracuse, New York, July 1992.

Lynton, E. "Scholarship Recognized." Unpublished manuscript, Carnegie Foundation for the Advancement of Teaching, Princeton, N.J., 1992.

Marchese, T. "Hearing Faculty Voices." *Change*, 1992, 24 (6), 4.

Rice, R. E. "The New American Scholar: Scholarship and the Purposes of the University." *Metropolitan Universities Journal*, 1991, 1 (4), 7–18.

Survey Research Laboratory. *An Overview of Results from the Virginia Faculty Survey*. Richmond: Survey Research Laboratory, Virginia Commonwealth University, 1991.

ROBERT M. DIAMOND *is assistant vice chancellor for instructional development and professor of instructional development, design, and evaluation at Syracuse University. He also is director of Changing Priorities in Higher Education, a project sponsored by the Lilly Endowment.*

The task of providing the proper climate and conditions for successful change is the central challenge confronting academic administrators. A clear mission statement centers the campus dialogue on the particular goals and objectives of the institution.

Instituting Change in the Faculty Reward System

Robert M. Diamond

Any modification in the promotion and tenure system requires a commitment to change from both the administration and the faculty. This investment creates shared ownership of the spirit of the initiative as well as of the final plan. Such partnership facilitates successful implementation.

Role of the Administration

The initial and primary role of the president and the chief academic officer is to provide leadership for the basic undertaking. Cochern (1992, p. 132) has described this aspect of administrative responsibility as follows:

> Faculty members need to be reassured by these individuals that this is not another log-rolling exercise and that their actions will be supported. Signs of strong leadership must be demonstrated so faculty members will join the movement. Leadership that bonds faculty and administrative efforts into a united front must be forthcoming. Administrators must be willing to support teacher-scholar activity, promote new teaching initiatives, and create imaginative ways to enhance teaching and learning. They must foster an attitude that stimulates the development of a quality teaching environment. Actions need to be taken that reduce the faculty's fear of evaluation.

In general, the administration has several distinct responsibilities in facilitating revision of the promotion and tenure process. First, *the administration must place revision of the promotion and tenure process on the*

NEW DIRECTIONS FOR HIGHER EDUCATION, no. 81, Spring 1993 © Jossey-Bass Publishers

institutional agenda. Action will not begin until a commitment to this activity is clearly understood at all levels of the academy. The need for change must be clearly articulated, and involvement in the process must be systematically encouraged. Administrators on many campuses have found that citation of data from *A National Study of Research Universities on the Balance Between Research and Undergraduate Teaching* (Gray, Froh, and Diamond, 1992) is an excellent way to begin a campuswide conversation about institutional priorities and the faculty reward system.

Second, *the administration must propose a process for change.* The task of changing the promotion and tenure system is far more complex and difficult than one might anticipate. The administration is responsible for providing the guidelines and general procedures of the process as well as for defining roles and establishing time lines.

Third, *the administration must facilitate the development of an appropriate institutional mission statement.* This statement of institutional purpose must be developed in such a way that it is understood and accepted, both in spirit and practice, by all major institutional constituents (faculty, administrators, students, and staff). While obviously limited in its detail, an institutional mission statement should (1) describe the desired institutional balance of teaching, research, and service activities; (2) identify major characteristics, strengths, and priorities of the institution; and (3) define the operational philosophy of the college or university.

The following examples—from St. Norbert College, DePere, Wisconsin, and the University of Tennessee, Knoxville—clearly demonstrate the differences among institutions and their mission statements.

> As a Catholic liberal arts college in the Norbertine tradition, the mission of St. Norbert College is to provide a superior education that is personally, intellectually, and spiritually challenging.

> As Tennessee's State University and landmark institution, the University of Tennessee, Knoxville, has a unique mission. UTK is the State's premier comprehensive institution, providing excellence in graduate and professional studies, selective baccalaureate programs, research, and creative activity and public service.

On many campuses the mission statement is rarely consulted, often vague, and of little use when specifics are needed. Of greater utility, particularly in the assessment of teaching, are statements that address specifically the expected attitudes and behaviors of administrators, faculty, and students. Documents such as the *Carolinian Creed* at the University of South Carolina, *Compact* at Syracuse University, and *Expectations* at the University of Tennessee contain specific references to the role of faculty in student advising, the treatment of students, and classroom responsibility.

Fourth, *the administration must understand the important roles that faculty, department chairs, and the academic discipline play in the change process.* Since it is the faculty who ultimately will write and implement revised guidelines and procedures for promotion and tenure, administrators should plan for faculty involvement from the outset. Administrators must be sensitive to the need for support at both the departmental and discipline levels. Faculty priorities are strongly influenced by disciplinary associations since faculty tend to identify themselves, first, as members of the community with whom they share scholarly interests. In a competitive national marketplace, the statements and agendas of professional disciplinary associations affect promotion and tenure guidelines. Faculty scholars' second loyalty is to their departments, where they work, develop support groups, and receive administrative guidance. It is, therefore, essential that faculty actively participate in the revision of promotion and tenure guidelines for their own departments. The role of the administration is to facilitate the process while supporting the right of different departments to develop their own appropriate criteria.

Fifth, *the administration must develop an active information program that systematically reinforces the importance of the project and describes its progress.* Administrators, including the president, academic officers, deans, and department chairs, must, whenever appropriate, publicly acknowledge the importance of the effort to revise faculty recognition and reward structures and provide regular progress reports. Constant support is essential during the difficult process of modifying the faculty reward system.

Role of Promotion and Tenure Committees

Much of the responsibility for program implementation rests with faculty serving on promotion and tenure committees, and this level is where many problems with the present system become most apparent. Stresses are most evident on cross-disciplinary committees, since such committees require faculty to make decisions about the performance of colleagues in fields in which they may not have scholarly expertise. Faculty in those fields where publication and research are not the primary currency can be placed at a distinct disadvantage. The problem is compounded by the erroneous belief of some faculty that teaching cannot be evaluated, which provides justification for giving teaching little weight in faculty assessment. As promotion and tenure criteria become both more specific and more diverse, an intensive education effort will be required for faculty serving on cross-disciplinary committees. Generally, faculty serving on promotion and tenure committees must

Understand fully the criteria used for the evaluation of each faculty member and the standards appropriate for the academic discipline and the specific activity involved (as greater diversity in assignments evolves, different criteria for promotion and tenure must be established)

Understand the range of techniques and assessment tools needed to properly evaluate teaching

Be willing to separate the criteria used for promotion and tenure in their own disciplines from those used in other fields when the faculty member under review is from another discipline

In short, for the process to succeed, each discipline must establish standards that are appropriate, clear, and measurable so that those in the field as well as colleagues in other disciplines can understand them. However the assessment criteria are revised to achieve greater appropriateness and fairness, they will require more flexibility from faculty serving on promotion and tenure committees than has been necessary in the past.

Process of Change

Review and revision of the promotion and tenure process on an individual campus involve four basic steps: (1) development of an institutional mission statement, (2) development of departmental and divisional mission statements in concert with the institutional statement, (3) development of departmental and divisional promotion and tenure guidelines and procedures based on the goals in these mission statements, (4) institutional review and approval of both mission statements and the faculty reward guidelines. As Figure 2.1 illustrates, each step requires input from a number of sources and extensive dialogue before a formal plan can be developed.

Development of an Institutional Mission Statement. Recent studies suggest that a productive campus culture exists when the faculty reward system is based on an institutional mission statement that establishes priorities for the campus and contributes to a working climate for students, faculty, and staff. Austin, Rice, and Splete (1991, p. 33) reported a correlation between high faculty morale and a clearly articulated institutional mission statement: "A college where faculty morale is high has a distinctive and easily identifiable institutional culture. Such a college has a clearly stated and frequently discussed mission that is widely understood and accepted across the institution. Ceremonies and symbols—such as convocations, campus architecture, and special traditions—are used to underscore and express the key values and goals contributing to the campus culture."

Regional, state, and professional accreditation statements can play a role in the development of institutional mission statements (particularly at state institutions) and of department- and division-level statements, where

Figure 2.1. The Process of Integrating
Faculty Rewards with Institutional Missions

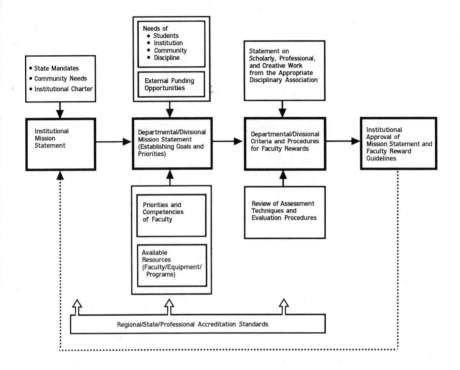

specific requirements must be met for certification or licensing. As Adam and Roberts (this volume) suggest, statements from professional associations may include specific promotion and tenure guidelines that will need to be considered for certification or accreditation purposes.

Development of Departmental and Divisional Mission Statements. Of more immediate significance in developing an operational promotion and tenure system is the discipline-based mission statement of the operational unit (department). Addressing the priorities of the institution and the specific goals of the academic unit, this statement can include references to specific programs, faculty roles, and the range of research activities considered desirable and appropriate. The departmental mission statement can also provide guidelines or criteria for assessing the unit as well as its constituent faculty. The following 1992 mission statement for the College of Business Administration at Drexel University is followed by eleven supporting objectives:

> The primary mission of the College of Business Administration is to provide men and women with the skills, knowledge, conceptual under-

standing, and ethical sensitivity to become innovative, responsible and accountable managers and leaders in the organizations they will join. In our desire to educate tomorrow's managers and leaders at all levels of society, we want to ensure the proper balance between technical skills and humanistic concerns so that our graduates will understand that they have an obligation to serve as well as to lead.

The College is committed academically to providing programs that address the managerial, administrative, and leadership needs of business, governmental, and nonprofit organizations. Research appropriate for these academic endeavors and tangentially related areas will be undertaken to maintain and enrich the intellectual capital of our faculty and contribute to the discipline-based body of knowledge. We will continually seek educational excellence through high quality, innovative curricula and an on-going faculty commitment to teaching, service, significant scholarly research and publication.

In developing a departmental or divisional mission statement, faculty must be sensitive to the needs of students, the goals and ideals of the institution, and the relationship between the institution and the community served. Other factors that must be considered include the focus and values of the academic discipline and the interests of external funding sources. The priorities and competencies of the faculty as well as existing and potential resources must also be taken into consideration. The Appendix of this volume includes selected sections from two departmental statements on faculty rewards that link institutional and departmental missions to the work of the faculty in those departments.

Development of Promotion and Tenure Guidelines and Procedures. Once the unit or department-specific mission statement is established, work can begin on developing discipline-specific criteria and procedures for use in the promotion and tenure process. To facilitate the process, broadened definitions of faculty work are being developed by disciplinary associations involved in Changing Priorities in Higher Education, a Syracuse University project sponsored by the Lilly Endowment. These documents provide lists of faculty activities from which departments can select those appropriate for their own particular contexts. Designed to facilitate discussion and to broaden the range of laudable faculty activities, the dissemination of these documents to faculty through their professional associations began in the 1992–1993 academic year.

Institutional Review and Approval. The final step in the process must be institutional approval of the departmental or divisional criteria and procedures. Ideally, the "final" plans continually undergo modifications as priorities, resources, and other key factors change.

Recommendations: A Framework for Change

Changes in the faculty reward system will not occur unless an institutional climate conducive to change is established and those affected by the changes—faculty, chairs, and deans—are involved in the change process.

Reconceptualization of faculty priorities requires a genuine commitment to change. All too often, major institutional initiatives have been characterized by extensive rhetoric and little action. Russell Edgerton (1992, pp. 14–15), president of the American Association of Higher Education (AAHE), in announcing the first AAHE-sponsored conference to address these issues, sounded a cautionary note:

> As in the case of assessment, the aroused interest in clarifying and shifting faculty priorities could unfold in different ways. We can envision a scenario in which there is a growing respect for dimensions of excellence beyond research, and a new appreciation for the "practice" of one's discipline . . . a culture in which all dimensions of professional and scholarly work are honored and peer reviewed. But we can also envision a nightmarish scenario . . . more reporting requirements, piles of evaluation data no one uses, prizes and rewards that have more to do with public relations than actual faculty motivation or improved performance.

The entire academic community must be actively involved in the change process. Unless the central administration, deans, department chairs, and individual faculty members have ownership of proposed modifications in the promotion and tenure process, adoption and implementation will be problematic. Ownership can come only when faculty play an active role in setting priorities, establishing criteria, and determining how revised promotion and tenure plans will be developed and assessed. Faculty involvement is necessary from the planning through the implementation and assessment stages if the change process is to be successful.

The difficulty of the process of changing promotion and tenure criteria will vary across academic areas and faculty. Although Gray, Froh, and Diamond's (1992) data show that the sciences, engineering, and some of the social sciences tend to be most comfortable with the status quo, change in these fields is essential for a number of reasons. First, in many instances, the emphasis on published research has had a detrimental impact on the quality of teaching and the scope of research conducted, on students' attitudes toward the science disciplines, and, consequently, on the numbers of students selecting science and engineering as careers and remaining in these departments once they have enrolled. As a result of a number of commissioned studies, the National Science Foundation has placed increased emphasis on teaching in its grant programs. Second, as federal resources for research continue to decline and as institutions begin to recognize that they can continue to support only their highest-quality research programs, pressure will increase in many departments to reestablish priorities and reassess the criteria by which faculty are evaluated.

Other disciplines, particularly the humanities, performing arts, most professional schools, and some of the social sciences, will be facing a different problem. Over the last decade or so, these fields have increasingly focused attention on publishable research in order to gain academic respectability. They will now be asked to refocus their efforts on activities that, until now, have received little attention. Younger faculty in these programs have been hired and rewarded as traditional researchers. The changes discussed here may be most stressful on the newest faculty if, at a critical time in their professional careers, the criteria by which they will be judged shift. For faculty who have received little support or training in teaching, this change may be particularly difficult to make. Laidlaw (1992, p. 4), in a report for the American Assembly of Collegiate Schools of Business, addressed these issues:

> In the late 1950s and early 1960s, major reports on the field of management education were sponsored by the Ford and Carnegie Foundations. Among the findings of those reports were that business schools were too vocational, lacked academic rigor, and taught subjects that were not founded in basic research. The Ford Foundation followed up its report with an investment of more than $30 million to upgrade the quality of doctoral programs, to incorporate research capability from other disciplines, and to create an environment that valued research as the basis for the development of the disciplines in management education. Our field has spent the last 30 years seeking academic respectability among university colleagues by emphasizing research and scholarship, often narrowly defined.

Members of another task force expressed concern that recognition of a broader range of scholarly activity might brand their faculty as "academic lightweights," thus dooming them to an academic underclass. Their draft report claims, however, that the benefits of such change will outweigh the negative implications by bringing greater congruence between the university mission and faculty priorities. The report argues that this congruence will lead to improved institutions, enhanced job placement of graduates, and restoration of public confidence in higher education. In addition, the committee members argue that the proposed changes will encourage greater diversity among faculty and support professional activities that benefit society and reduce faculty stress.

The criteria used for determining promotion and tenure must be context-

specific. Although overall procedures and general statements from different programs or schools may have much in common, there is significant variation among them in terms of the criteria used and the weight given to specific activities under consideration for recognition and reward. There are significant differences across institutions and across departments in the same discipline in terms of missions, goals, and objectives. In a recent meeting of faculty from the social sciences on a single campus, it was impossible to reach agreement on whether writing a textbook should be considered a "scholarly" activity and, if so, what documentation would be required to substantiate the scholarly nature of the endeavor. Some faculty claimed that the activity represents a teaching function, while others asserted, particularly if the text was written for an audience other than college students, that the activity should be considered a service function. The disagreement becomes even more striking when faculty from different types of institutions or from different disciplines consider this kind of question. As a result, institutions addressing these issues typically will find the promotion and tenure materials of other institutions to be of limited use without discussion and modification.

Development of unit or departmental statements and criteria for assessing faculty work is a far more time-consuming and labor-intensive task than might at first be anticipated. What can be shared are procedures, general models for the statements, documents that provide a range of alternatives such as disciplinary statements on the professional work of faculty, and approaches to assessment and documentation. The particulars must be developed locally for use in that context.

The Faculty Reward System Must Change

Colleges and universities must change, and in order for change to occur, those of us in higher education must modify what we do. A chorus of voices from the public and private sectors is calling for a shift in priorities, and our most important clients—our students—are demanding it. The question is how significant a role we, as faculty and administrators, want to play. We can sit back and mildly protest the status quo until frustrated government officials or external accreditation agencies define for us what we shall do and how we shall do it, or we can take a proactive role in shaping our future. Administrators and faculty must direct the process and participate in the many conversations that will be necessary to negotiate changes in the faculty reward system. The initial step of this process must be to address faculty priorities as determined by the promotion and tenure system. Unless the criteria by which faculty are recognized and rewarded are modified, the nature of faculty activities will remain constant. Administrators must encourage and facilitate the change process, and they must understand their key role in establishing a receptive climate for change.

Higher education has for too long been able to establish its own agenda. This luxury simply can no longer be maintained.

References

Austin, A., Rice, R. E., and Splete, A. *A Good Place to Work: Sourcebook for the Academic Workplace.* Washington, D.C.: Council of Independent Colleges, 1991.

Cochern, L. *Publish or Perish: The Wrong Issue.* Cape Girardeau, Mo.: Step Up, Inc., 1992.

Edgerton, R. "AAHE's New Forum on Faculty Roles and Rewards Launches Its First Conference." *AAHE Bulletin,* 1992, *45* (1).

Gray, P. J., Froh, R. C., and Diamond, R. M. *A National Study of Research Universities on the Balance Between Research and Undergraduate Teaching.* Syracuse, N.Y.: Center for Instructional Development, Syracuse University, 1992.

Laidlaw, W. K. *Defining Scholarly Work in Management Education.* St. Louis: American Assembly of Collegiate Schools of Business, 1992.

ROBERT M. DIAMOND is assistant vice chancellor for instructional development and professor of instructional development, design, and evaluation at Syracuse University. He also is director of Changing Priorities in Higher Education, a project sponsored by the Lilly Endowment.

A constellation of terms is necessary to describe the work of faculty,
because faculty do different things and view what they do from
different perspectives.

Differences Among the Disciplines

Bronwyn E. Adam, Alton O. Roberts

Following the publication of *Scholarship Reconsidered: Priorities for the Professoriate* (Boyer, 1990), much debate ensued about the nature of the process and products of "scholarship." As the dialogue has continued within and among disciplines in the academy, the complexity of the question of what constitutes scholarly work has become clear. Boyer's text, along with Rice's (1991) proposal for a four-part formulation of scholarship, struck a cord with academics and seemed a productive place to begin rethinking what it means to call oneself a scholar. Efforts to rethink traditional definitions of scholarship are underway nationwide at conferences, within disciplines, and on individual campuses. Some in higher education have resisted this approach, preferring instead to seek actions that elevate the status of teaching and professional service or outreach. One national initiative to rethink the nature of scholarship has focused on the academic discipline as the place where the general term *scholarship* can appropriately be given a context-specific definition.

In 1991, with funding from the Lilly Endowment and the Fund for the Improvement of Postsecondary Education, the Center for Instructional Development at Syracuse University invited twenty scholarly societies, learned associations, and accreditation agencies to participate in a project to define what faculty in the respective fields consider scholarly work. The project supported the work of task forces convened by the professional or disciplinary associations. Task forces consisted of faculty scholars, representative of the various constituencies within the fields of study, who met and drafted statements outlining the range of activities that faculty members pursue in the name of discipline-based scholarship.

What follows in this chapter are excerpts from five of those statements, from scholarly societies and learned associations representing the fields of

NEW DIRECTIONS FOR HIGHER EDUCATION, no. 81, Spring 1993   © Jossey-Bass Publishers

history, management and business, chemistry, and geography and a consortium of accreditation agencies and professional associations representing the arts. With minor adaptations, we reproduce the statements as completely as possible here given space constraints, while excising redundancies. Many similarities between the documents are apparent. All of the statements begin with some consideration of the work of Boyer and Rice; moreover, the collaborative nature of this project encouraged the task force members to examine one another's statements and to incorporate the work of their colleagues in synergistic ways. Although the numerous similarities are noteworthy, the differences among these statements are perhaps more interesting, for they tell us much about the differences among the disciplines.

At first, the differences among disciplines seem to be centered on language or terminology. But surface-level differences signal deeper differences in methodologies and values. It is not simply that faculty in different fields identify their activities by different names; rather, they do different things in different ways and for different reasons. For example, some disciplines value professional service or outreach activities because they serve a critical function in the life and development of the field. The statement reproduced here from the American Chemical Society addresses this value. In contrast, teaching is crucial in geography because undergraduates rarely come to college committed to the study of geography. The continuation of geography as a discipline depends directly on the strength of undergraduate instruction. Similarly, the production or making of art is central to the arts disciplines. Creation, as process and product, is the essence of art. Thus, making new things is central to the work of artist-scholars, but media and methodology differ across arts disciplines, and that which is made is not always tangible. In the arts, complexities abound.

Language theorists tell us that when we struggle to name something, the difficulty signals a deeper issue than that of "words." It is not simply that we use different names for different things. Scholarship, research, intellectual production, intellectual contribution, creative work, creative act, creative process, making art, doing research, professional work, scholarly work, the work of the professoriate—all of these terms name and assign different values to what faculty members do in the academic disciplines. "Scholars" are not all the same. The disciplines differ in deep and substantive ways from one another, and it follows that they differ in the ways in which they define what faculty do and what they dream of doing. The following statements demonstrate those differences.

Faculty Work in History

Following is an excerpt from *Redefining Historical Scholarship* (American Historical Association [AHA] Ad Hoc Committee on Redefining Scholarly Work, 1992):

Despite considerable differences in institutional missions and goals, most American colleges and universities agree on the basic criteria for faculty tenure and promotion decisions: the documentation and evaluation of research, teaching, and service. Although the relative weight given to each of the three criteria varies considerably from institution to institution, critics maintain that too much emphasis is now placed on the research component, with the other two relegated to considerably lesser if not irrelevant status. For example, Ernest Boyer of the Carnegie Foundation for the Advancement of Teaching maintains that this equation of scholarship with research and publication, while perhaps having served many faculty and institutions well over the years, has perpetuated narrow individual and institutional priorities at odds with the broader interest of faculty and with the varied needs of colleges and universities today. In *Scholarship Reconsidered: Priorities for the Professoriate*, Boyer (1990, pp. 15–16) argues that "a wide gap now exists between the myth and the reality of academic life. Almost all colleges pay lip service to the trilogy of teaching, research, and service, but when it comes to making judgments about professional performance, the three rarely are assigned equal merit. . . . The time has come to move beyond the tired old 'teaching versus research' debate and give the familiar and honorable term 'scholarship' a broader, more capacious meaning, one that brings legitimacy to the full scope of academic work."

This debate over priorities is not discipline-specific but extends across the higher education community. Nevertheless, each discipline has specific concerns and problems. For history, the privilege given to the monograph in promotion and tenure has led to the undervaluing of other activities central to the life of the discipline—writing textbooks, developing courses and curricula, documentary editing, museum exhibitions, and film projects to name but a few. Despite a number of efforts within recent years to give greater recognition to such work, a traditional, hierarchical conceptualization of what constitutes historical scholarship, based on the German university model, continues to dominate and restrict our profession's rewards structure. There is little recognition of the diverse interests and talents of today's historians or of the changes that they undergo over the course of their careers. The situation is unlikely to change until we as a profession consciously rethink the fundamental meaning of historical scholarship and the role of the historian as scholar today.

While frustration over the academic rewards structure may be the catalyst, a reexamination of the meaning of scholarship has much larger implications for the profession—if scholarly activity is central to the work of our profession, then how we define scholarship determines what it means to be a historian and who is part of the historical community. The AHA defines the history profession in broad, encompassing terms, but is that definition meaningful as long as only certain kinds of work are valued and deemed scholarly within our discipline? If the historical profession is a broad community of individuals committed to "teaching, researching, writing, or otherwise providing or disseminating historical knowledge and understanding" (AHA Ad Hoc Committee on the Future of the AHA, 1988, p. 1), then the virtually exclusive identification of historical scholarship with the monograph is inappropriate and unfairly undervalues the work of a significant portion of professional historians. Just how many historians are excluded by a narrow definition of scholarship? According to data from a 1985–1986 study conducted by the American Council of Learned Societies, only 41.8 percent of historians surveyed have published one or more scholarly books or monographs during their careers.

AHA Ad Hoc Committee. Within this context, the AHA agreed in 1991 to participate in two initiatives that call for the development of discipline-specific redefinitions of scholarly work. The first, conducted by Syracuse University and supported by the Fund for the Improvement of Postsecondary Education and the Lilly Endowment, focuses on enhancing the status of teaching within the faculty rewards system. Eighteen professional associations are taking part in this effort. In the second project, eleven professional associations have agreed to undertake a variety of efforts to increase recognition for scholarship-based professional service. The cosponsors of this project are the National Association of State Universities and Land Grant Colleges, the University of Maryland at College Park, and Wayne State University, with support from the Johnson Foundation.

The association's agreement to take part in these two projects rested on five assumptions:

1. Problems associated with the faculty rewards system are not discipline-specific. Hence, individual disciplines and their associations may be a good place to start, but they cannot be expected to bring about reform single-handedly. Similar initiatives must be launched within higher education associations and college and university administration if there is to be any substantial change.

2. The AHA's role should not be to prescribe a certain formula but rather to suggest alternative ways of conceptualizing scholarly work and to provide examples of the different ways in which history departments have addressed this issue. The emphasis should be on what "can be" considered scholarship, not what "must be" or "is." Any statement from the association must be adaptable to the varied needs of different departments and institutions and leave room for individual and institutional choices.

3. A redefinition of scholarly work should not diminish or undermine historical research but rather extend and enhance it. Nor should a redefinition lead to a competitive situation—the relationship of research to other scholarly work should be viewed as complementary not competitive. Research—as well as teaching—remains at the heart of the profession.

4. The association's concern is with historians' activities that relate directly to their research and teaching, broadly defined, and not with public

service, civic involvement, or other service to their institutions and communities. While the latter are valuable and should be encouraged, they do not draw upon the historian's professional or disciplinary expertise and cannot be characterized as scholarly.

5. Reform efforts should focus on increasing flexibility within the system and avoid the imposition of additional requirements on already overburdened tenure track faculty. Moreover, priorities should change concomitantly in institutional support for faculty. The point should be to change priorities and increase options, not to demand more.

Conceptual Framework. An essay by Eugene Rice, Antioch College, titled "The New American Scholar: Scholarship and the Purposes of the University" (Rice, 1991), provided the context for the ad hoc committee's work. The Rice essay provides an alternative conceptualization of scholarly work: He proposes that the trilogy of research, teaching, and service be abandoned in favor of a more inclusive four-part definition of scholarship. In so doing, the discussion broadens from issues of balance within the campus-defined function of professor to the larger roles and obligations of the scholar. Drawing on the work of Ernest Boyer, Sandra E. Elman, Ernest Lynton, Lee Shulman, and others, Rice breaks scholarship down into four distinct yet interrelated components: (1) advancement of knowledge—essentially original research; (2) integration of knowledge—synthesizing and reintegrating knowledge, revealing new patterns of meaning and new relationships between the parts and the whole; (3) application of knowledge—professional practice directly related to an individual's scholarly specialization; and (4) transformation of knowledge through teaching—including pedagogical content knowledge and discipline-specific educational theory. As Rice (1991, p. 6) concluded,

> We know that what is being proposed challenges a hierarchical arrangement of monumental proportions—a status system that is firmly fixed in the consciousness of the present faculty and the academy's organizational policies and practices. What is being called for is a broader, more open field where these different forms of scholarship can interact, inform, and enrich one another, and faculty can follow their interests, build on their strengths, and be rewarded for what they spend most of their scholarly energy doing. All faculty ought to be scholars in this broader sense, deepening their preferred approaches to knowing but constantly pressing, and being pressed by peers, to enlarge their scholarly capacities and encompass other—often contrary—ways of knowing.

An Expanded Definition of Historical Scholarship. The ad hoc committee applied this framework to the history discipline, using as a starting point the following passage from *Statement on Standards of Professional Conduct* (AHA, 1992, p. 5): "Scholarship, the uncovering and exchange of new information and the shaping of interpretations, is basic to the activities of the historical profession. The profession communicates with students in text-books and classrooms; to other scholars and the general public in books, articles, exhibits, films, and historic sites and structures; and to decision-makers in memoranda and testimony."

The description is clearly broader than the traditional definition of scholarship as original research, and it provided the committee with the basis for developing an expanded list of activities appropriate for consideration under a more inclusive tenure and promotion system. The list that follows is basically an inventory of activities that *can* be scholarly but does not address when a particular activity is scholarly and when it is not—that is an issue of evaluation, as discussed below. For example, teaching can be a scholarly activity but all teaching is not scholarly in nature.

Using the Rice formulation of scholarship, the committee proposes that within history

1. The advancement of knowledge includes original research—based on manuscript and printed sources, material culture, oral history interviews, or other source materials—published in the form of a monograph or refereed journal article or disseminated through a paper or lecture given at a meeting or conference or through a museum exhibition or other project or program; documentary or critical editions; and translations.

2. The integration of knowledge includes synthesis of scholarship—published in a review essay (journal or anthology), textbook, newsletter, popular history, magazine, encyclopedia, newspaper, or other form of pub-lication or disseminated through a paper or lecture given at a meeting or conference or through a museum exhibition, film, or other public program; and edited anthologies, journals, or series of volumes composed of the work of other scholars.

3. The application of knowledge includes public history, specifically: public programming (exhibitions, tours, and so on) in museums and other cultural and educational institutions, consulting and providing expert testi-mony on public policy and other matters, participation in film and other media projects, writing and compiling institutional and other histories, historic preservation and cultural resource management, administration and management of historical organizations and institutions, archival adminis-tration and the creation of bibliographies and data bases; professional services (editing journals and newsletters, organizing scholarly meetings, and so on); and community service drawing directly upon scholarship—through state humanities councils (for example, public lectures), history day competitions, and so on.

4. The transformation of knowledge through teaching includes student mentoring and advising; research, writing, and consulting in history educa-tion and in other disciplines allied to history; development of courses, curricula, visual materials, and teaching materials (including edited antholo-

gies, textbooks, and software)—implemented in the classroom or disseminated through publications (books, professional newsletter articles, and so
on), papers (annual meetings, teaching conferences, and so on), or nonprint
forms; organization and participation in collaborative content-based programs (workshops, seminars, and so on) with the schools; participation in
developing and evaluating advanced placement and other forms of assessment; and museum exhibitions, catalogues, lectures, film, radio, and so on—
public programs as forms of teaching.

While the charge to the committee was to develop a discipline-specific
definition of scholarly work, the above formulation would be applicable as
well to interdisciplinary work by historians. The committee did not address,
however, the relative value of or weight that should be given to such work.

Weighting, Documentation, and Evaluation. As indicated earlier, this
list of activities should not be viewed as prescriptive or definitive but rather
as suggestive of how historical scholarship can be redefined to be more
inclusive and multidimensional. While the breakdown provides a good
starting point for departmental reassessment of promotion and tenure
criteria, any such effort must also take into account the mission and goals of
the individual department and the institution of which it is a part. Even if a
department adopts the redefinition, it must still determine for itself the
appropriate balance among the four components an the relative weight to be
assigned to each. A central question that every department should address
is whether there is a single mix or balance that each individual within the
department must achieve or whether there is room for individuals to weight
categories of work differently, as long as the department overall achieves a
balance consistent with its mission.

But agreeing on an appropriate definition of scholarly work is only the
first step—implementation is impossible without the development of appropriate strategies for documentation and evaluation. Work that cannot be
documented and evaluated does not merit reward. But how is the work to
be documented? It is relatively simple to provide copies of books or articles
produced as part of one's research, but how is an innovative classroom
activity or a museum exhibit documented? Advocates of the redefinition of
scholarly work maintain that scholarship is strengthened when other activities are included, but it is difficult to demonstrate scholarly quality and rigor
when documentation involves no more than counting or identifying. New
forms of documentation such as portfolios and reflective essays must be
implemented.

Attention also must be given to peer review and evaluation. Who will
evaluate this scholarship? Do you require outside reviewers for teaching as
you do for research? How do you secure the reviewers needed to evaluate
work outside the usual expertise of faculty, such as for evaluation? Ernest
Lynton (1992) has suggested that evaluation criteria might include the
expertise informing the choices made, the degree of innovation manifested

in the activity, the difficulty of the task accomplished, and the scope and importance of the activity. For an example of how documentation and evaluation has been addressed for a nontraditional form of scholarship (museum exhibitions), see Schlereth (1989).

As each department or institution develops or adopts standards and criteria appropriate to its own mission and goals, the problem of transferability from one institution to another arises—will a scholar with nontraditional credentials find his or her mobility restricted? It is likely, for example, that the most prestigious research universities will continue to weight those activities classified under "advancement of knowledge" very heavily in appointment and promotion decisions. Thus senior members of a department have an obligation to counsel junior colleagues not only about the criteria for promotion in his or her own institution but also about the realities that govern advancement in the profession beyond that institution.

Case Studies in Faculty Roles and Rewards. For a discussion of these tenure and promotion issues within the specific context of the history profession, see the appended October and December 1989 and June 1991 issues of *Organization of American Historians Council of Chairs Newsletter.* These newsletters provide case studies of policies and procedures at eight very different public and private colleges and universities, including a two-year senior college, three general baccalaureate institutions, two comprehensive institutions, and two doctoral-level universities. Moreover, the departments vary in terms of the highest degree offered—five offer the B.A., two the M.A., and one the Ph.D.—and in size—from ten to nearly thirty faculty each. These case studies provide both valuable illustrations of alternative faculty rewards systems and direction in addressing documentation and evaluation questions.

The members of the AHA Ad Hoc Committee on Redefining Scholarly Work are Robert A. Blackey, AHA vice president for teaching, California State University, San Bernardino; Blanche Wiesen Cook, AHA vice president for research, John Jay College of Criminal Justice, City University of New York; Susan Socolow, AHA vice president for the profession, Emory University; Philip V. Scarpino, Indiana University–Purdue University at Indianapolis, representing the Organization of American Historians; Noel J. Stowe, Arizona State University, representing the National Council on Public History; James Powell, Syracuse University; J. Rodger Sharp, Syracuse University; Carlin Barton, University of Massachusetts; Gerald F. Linderman, University of Michigan; David Miller, Carnegie-Mellon University; and James B. Gardner, AHA Deputy Executive Director (ex officio).

Faculty Work in Management and Business

Following is an excerpt from the AACSB's *Defining Scholarly Work in Management Education* (Laidlaw, 1992):

Background. In most universities and colleges in the United States, faculty promotion and tenure decisions are based on criteria involving research, teaching, and service. Depending on the historical roots and thrust of the institution, the weights assigned to these criteria often vary. There is nothing discipline-specific about the relative importance of these criteria as they relate to the evaluation of academic work. Rather, the debate about their importance embraces all of higher education, especially today, when there is considerable criticism from the public and other professions that research receives too much of the emphasis. The situation in management education is no different, and if one looks at the roots of the problem, the current situation is understandable. In the late 1950s and early 1960s, major reports on the field of management education were sponsored by the Ford and Carnegie foundations. Among the findings of those reports were that business schools were too vocational, lacked academic rigor, and taught subjects that were not founded in basic research. The Ford Foundation followed up its report with an investment of more than $30 million to upgrade the quality of doctoral programs, to incorporate research capability from other disciplines, and to create an environment that valued research as the basis for development of the disciplines in management education. Our field has spent the last thirty years seeking academic respectability among university colleagues by emphasizing research and scholarship, often narrowly defined.

The final report of the American Assembly of Collegiate Schools of Business (AACSB) Task Force on Faculty Research (1987) defined research in the following way: "Research must be written, be subject to scrutiny and criticism by one's peers and extend the boundaries of current knowledge." The committee went on to provide categories of research to fit the definition: (1) theoretical or empirical "discovery" research, including integrative and interdisciplinary research that makes new discoveries by linking avenues of thought across diverse disciplines; (2) applied research in which one applies others' discovery research to new contexts, fields, industries, firms, nations, time periods, and so on; (3) written teaching cases accompanied by an instructor's manual, which can be scrutinized and critiqued by one's peers; (4) computer software that is circulated and not totally proprietary; (5) textbooks and other pedagogical writing that extend the boundaries of knowledge, circulate, and can be critiqued.

Written material (such as some consulting reports) that is proprietary would not meet the definition and thus would not qualify as research. Written cases without a published instructor's manual would also not qualify. Such material lacks the necessary ingredients of scrutiny by one's peers and of allowing public determination of how the research extends the boundaries of current knowledge.

We are not implying that all business schools should encourage or reward all five types of research listed. Indeed, it is proper that some schools will choose to reward or pursue only a subset of these types, depending on the clienteles they serve. Thus, some schools may choose an emphasis on discovery research at the expense of encouraging textbook and case writing; others may legitimately do the reverse. In fact, schools that need to revive their faculty research activities ought to consider that legitimate research, as we have defined it, includes translating other people's discovery research into a form that makes it applicable to practitioners. There is no presumption here that only discovery research counts or is appropriate. Rather, we suggest that every AACSB-accredited school incorporate in its standards for tenure and promotion a requirement that faculty members engage in at least one of these five types of research.

In April 1991, the AACSB membership approved new standards of accreditation, which require that a "formal, periodic review process should exist for reappointment, promotion, and tenure decisions that produces results consistent with the school's mission and objectives" (AACSB, 1991, pp. 12–13). The standards point out that among the "criteria used for evaluation, attention should be given to course development, effective teaching, and instructional innovation" (p. 13). Another standard calls for the school to "support continuing faculty intellectual development and renewal" (p. 13). The standard on "intellectual contributions" requires "faculty members [to] make intellectual contributions on a continuing basis appropriate to the mission of the school. The outputs of intellectual contributions should be available for public scrutiny by academic peers or practitioners" (p. 31). The standard goes on to interpret the components of intellectual contributions as the creation of new knowledge (basic scholarship); the application, transfer, and interpretation of knowledge to improve management practice and teaching (applied scholarship); and the enhancement of the educational value of instructional efforts of the institution or discipline (instructional developments).

As a result of the work of the Accreditation Project Committee, and following up on the work of Porter and McKibbin (1988), the AACSB leadership felt it important to conduct an inquiry into the nature of Ph.D. programs. Since those programs are such an important factor not only in developing knowledge and research skills but also in establishing the basic value system of faculty members, it seemed logical that major reform in management education would not take place unless it started with the products of the doctoral programs. Of particular interest was the preparation for teaching offered by doctoral programs and the relative importance between teaching and research implied by the values imparted in Ph.D. programs.

Current Project. In the fall of 1991, the AACSB Board of Directors agreed to participate in a project, titled Defining Scholarly Work, of national scope, which is coordinated by Syracuse University with support from the Fund for the Improvement of Postsecondary Education (FIPSE) and the Lilly Endowment. The project focuses on enhancing the status of teaching within the faculty reward system and, ultimately, looking at opportunities for changing the promotion/tenure and merit systems. Eighteen academic/professional associations are participating in this project. The National Study on the Perceived Balance Between Undergraduate Teaching and Research, which was part of this project, demonstrated that all groups of faculty and administrators desire a balanced integration of research and teaching. The perception, however, is that the next group higher in the academic hierarchy places greater value on research. Perceptions, then, appear to be a major barrier to changing policies for evaluating faculty performance.

Data available from the national study show that differences exist by discipline within business schools. For example, economics, marketing, and finance faculty would like to see more emphasis placed on research, while management, management information systems, and accounting faculty would like to see the emphasis moved more toward teaching. Recognizing that differences between disciplines are important, and that the missions of different schools create significantly different environments for evaluating research and teaching, the AACSB board agreed to participate in the next stage of this effort, which was to convene a task force during April 1992 to determine how best to evaluate the portfolios of activities faculty members may present as evidence that they engage in various kinds of scholarship and teaching activities.

AACSB agreed to participate in the Syracuse project for several reasons: (1) Not all of the problems associated with faculty reward systems are discipline-specific. Hence, individual disciplines and their association may be a good place to start, but they cannot be expected to bring about reform single-handedly. Similar initiatives must be launched within higher education associations and college and university administrations if there is to be any substantial change. (2) AACSB's role should not be to prescribe a certain formula, but rather to suggest alternative ways in which schools of business may address this issue. Any statement from the assembly must be adaptable to the varied needs of different departments and institutions. (3) Reform efforts should focus on increasing flexibility within this system. (4) The faculty reward system is flawed, but it is not clear how. (5) There must be a "product" as a result of faculty work that must be replicable and available for external evaluation.

Charged with redefining scholarship in order to incorporate aspects into teaching and service activities, the task force produced the following definitions supplemented by examples. The committee used as its basis the interpretations for intellectual contributions from Section I, item C1 of the new accreditation standards:

Basic scholarship: the creation of new knowledge. Outputs from basic scholarship activities include publication in refereed journals, research monographs, scholarly books, chapters in scholarly books, proceedings from scholarly meetings, papers presented at academic meetings, publicly available research seminars. Discovery research, the testing of theories, is included along with developing theories based on case development. Interdisciplinary work across fields, for example, environmental studies and management, or language studies and international business, are also included.

Applied scholarship: the application, transfer, and interpretation of knowledge to approved management practice and teaching. Outputs from applied service scholarship activities include publication in professional journals, professional presentations, public/trade/practitioner journals, in-house book reviews, and papers presented at faculty workshops. Also included are writing of cases to illustrate existing theories, adapting pure research of others into text, service to community (for example, internships and case enrichment), interpreting real work experience to classroom use that is generalizable and reusable, and interdisciplinary work across fields such as environmental studies in management or language studies and international business.

Instructional development: the enhancement of the educational value of instructional efforts of the institution or discipline. Output from instructional development activities include textbooks, publications in pedagogical journals, written cases with instructional materials, instructional software, and publicly available materials describing the design and implementation of new courses. Also included are executive education course teaching, internships supervised by faculty, and materials used to enhance student learning, for example, for advising and mentoring students and for assessment. In addition, developing new curriculum materials or support materials to be used by others (slides, video presentations, computer software, teachers' manuals) are included.

The following additional observations were made by task force members. Because management education is multidisciplinary in nature and because the accreditation standards are now mission-driven, there is a need for a range of options for schools. The fact that different institutions have different values necessitates varied approaches to evaluation. Such evaluations should relate to accreditation, faculty development, and continuous improvement. It is important to avoid putting a system in place that would lead to stagnation.

For true change to be made, faculty must play a dominant role. And decisions would be better if they were program-based, rather than simply discipline-based. A list of indicators or options of scholarship might be used to challenge colleges to select a set consistent with their mission and then demonstrate how they meet those indicators.

A task force was formed consisting of representatives from six of the schools involved in an earlier phase of the Lilly project, as well as individuals with significant experience in the new formulation of standards and procedures for AACSB accreditation. Its members are Joseph Alutto, dean, Ohio State University; George Burman, dean, Syracuse University; Dennis Epple, Ph.D., Carnegie-Mellon University; Lyn Goodridge, dean, University of New Hampshire; William Hasler, dean, University of California at Berkeley; Barbara Jones, dean, Prairie View A&M University; Edwin Miller, Ph.D., University of Michigan; Thomas O'Brien, dean, University of Massachusetts at Amherst; and Willis Sheftall, dean, Morehouse College. In addition, William Setten represented Richard D. Irwin, who has made funds available to help meet some of the costs associated with this project. Joining from the AACSB staff were Milton Blood, director of accreditation, and William K. Laidlaw, Jr., executive vice president.

Faculty Work in the Arts

Following is an excerpt from *The Work of Arts Faculties in Higher Education* (Interdisciplinary Task Force, 1992):

About This Document. Work in the various arts disciplines has a vital role in higher education throughout the United States. As both higher education and the arts evolve, old challenges reformulate themselves, and new challenges arise. Increasingly, choices are made while contexts change rapidly. Over time, policies, procedures, and personnel decisions define the scope, depth, and effectiveness of each institution's work. In this context, few decisions are as important as those made about faculty.

The centrality of faculty issues has caused groups representing various academic disciplines to participate in a national project to consider the elements of faculty work. Each disciplinary group agreed to define and present its own elements and to explain their interrelationships in teaching, creative activity, research, and service. This document considers the arts in general and covers specifically the fields of architecture, art and design, dance, film and video, landscape architecture, music, and theater. It is a consensus document completed after review by over one thousand programs in colleges, universities, and independent schools of the arts.

Purposes. Intellectual and creative powers are central to the work of all faculty. However, intellectual and creative activities, formats, and agendas can be employed for different purposes and to different effect both within and across disciplines. Our purposes are to explain the basic nature of intellectual and creative work in the arts and to present lists of responsibilities undertaken by arts faculties, thereby assisting development of local definitions and policies that support faculty work in the arts. We explain basic themes and premises, explore major analytical issues, annotate typical faculty activities, and provide advice about decision making in institutional settings. Our analyses and recommendations are derived from the nature of work both *in* and *about* art. Our approach is intended to open possibilities for new thinking and new arrangements about the value of a broad range of activities that arts faculty undertake. We intend to encourage communication and understanding that assist local prioritization and evaluation.

Terminology. For purposes of this document, the term *arts* normally refers to all of the arts and arts-related disciplines, and their subdisciplines. The term *unit* is used to designate the entire program in a particular arts discipline; thus, in specific cases *unit* refers to free-standing institutions and to departments or schools that are part of larger institutions.

Making art indicates the creation of an entirely new work of art or the creative process applied to performance. These activities may be mixed in a single effort, and they may be collaborative or individual. Our use of *making art* always indicates applications of knowledge, skills, and intellectual technique.

The word *work* is used in title and text because it provides an umbrella for the different types of faculty activities essential to the arts in higher education. This umbrella is necessary because definitions of such terms as creative activity, research, scholarship, teaching, and service can be narrow or broad. For example, when broadly defined, research can include the process of making a work of art: A search for the new is involved. When more narrow definitions based on science or humanities methodologies are applied, making art is not research, although research of scientific or humanistic types may be involved in the total art-making process. The word *work* enables respect and use of both narrow and broad definitions as institutions, organizations, and individuals may determine in specific circumstances. Whether broad or narrow, our use of *work* always indicates intense use of mind.

Standard descriptions of faculty work mention three areas. Two of these areas—teaching and service—seem to have common use throughout higher education. The third area involving each faculty member's individual and collaborative work in one or more fields is more problematic. Across the nation, various terminologies cover various concepts without much title or content consistency. The project task force struggled with this issue from numerous perspectives. As a result, the text uses *creative work and research* to name the third area. This formulation, while not perfect, has utility, especially if it is understood to express interrelationships rather than polarities. Creative work is an element of research; research is an element of creative work. Thus, making art and studying about art are both deeply intellectual. Our use of the word *intellectual* covers both of these activities.

Fundamentals. Definitions and policies concerning the work of the faculty are best developed and applied in terms of the specific mission, goals, and objectives present at each institution. Specific goals and objectives of various disciplinary programs may create a multiplicity of unique approaches and needs on a single campus. The following information and analysis should be used only in the contexts of and in relation to specific purposes, programs, and resources.

The Powers of Art. Works of art are powerful. They speak through the emotions. They reflect and stimulate passionate engagement. They provide cultural identity and engender civilization. But behind these powers lies the magic of aesthetic effect produced by organization, logic, and intellectual process. These attributes and conditions make the creation, interpretation, performance, and study of art central to higher education. It is the arts faculty, however, that provides the knowledge, skills, expertise, and long-term inspiration that keep the powers of art and our understandings about them at the highest possible levels.

The Arts as Disciplines. In some sense, all disciplines in higher education are concerned with discovering how things work, with what happened, with making new things, and with what things mean. Influenced by varying missions, goals, and objectives, institutions, schools, and programs, the disciplines themselves, and their component activities, arrange priorities for these concerns in different ways at different times.

At base, the arts disciplines are all concerned with making new things. To make art is to compile a variety of elements into a unique arrangement. This happens every time a work of art is created or performed. But work in the arts disciplines goes much further. There are concerns with what happened, as revealed through the history of various art forms, with how things work in terms of internal mechanisms that generate artistic effectiveness, and with what things mean both in artistic terms and from other disciplinary perspectives. Over centuries, pursuit of these concerns has produced systematic, transmittable bodies of knowledge. The continued creation, discovery, storage, and transfer of this knowledge are the primary concern of arts faculty.

Work in Art. Approaching the process of making art means approaching a realm that is complex, open-ended, usually without empirical objectives, and often expressed in terms that are neither verbal nor mathematical. Creation, interpretation, and performance all involve using the communication systems and media of an art form to produce a work. Each work, whether new or recreated, is a small universe of meaning with its own internal logics whether standing alone or used in juxtaposition with other works, events, and functions. Each work also reflects and produces multiple universes of meaning as it relates to the external world where it is produced, received, and studied.

Work About *Art*. The study of art involves a vast complex of functions, purposes, and efforts. Each art form has its own history and body of analytical technique. Each has rich connections with general history and with the analytical techniques of the sciences and the humanities. And the arts as a group can be studied through disciplines ranging from aesthetics to management.

Critical Interrelationships. Taken as a whole, arts activities in higher education cover a broad range of work *in* and *about* art. Whatever objectives, definitions, and approaches are used, many critical interrelationships exist between the making of art on the one hand, and the study of completed work through research and scholarship on the other. Although the specifics of these interrelationships are defined and brought to bear in different ways to accomplish specific artistic, educational, and scholarly goals, the interrelationships themselves cannot be broken. Art-making processes, finished works of art, and research and scholarship about the arts and their impact are interdependent. Pursuit of any one creates some sort of relationship with the others.

Intellectual work involves creation, discovery, analysis, integration, synthesis, application, and evaluation. Weightings and arrangements of these elements vary across disciplines and across the activities, responsibilities, and perspectives associated with specific disciplines. In the arts, it is often a challenge to isolate and quantify these elements in analyses of faculty activities. Work in and about art, whether applied to teaching, individual activity in a field, or service, involves interrelationships among these elements that vary greatly within generic types of work. This is particularly true when creative activity, research, scholarship, teaching, and service are defined broadly.

Approaches and Perspectives. Making new things, considering what happened, discovering how things work, and searching for meaning become the basis for complex applications as individual institutions, faculties, and faculty members take various approaches to making art, studying art, and presenting art. When considering these approaches, it is important to make distinctions between mediums and methodologies. Each arts discipline has its own media and its own sets of processes and techniques. Some processes and techniques are shared among the arts in general and some are discipline-specific. Specific works of art may combine the processes and techniques of two or more arts disciplines. And some art forms—architecture, landscape architecture, and design, for example—have close relationships with a variety of applied sciences.

Further, there are numerous perspectives for studying art. Singly, or in combination, these perspectives can address how things work, what happened, what things mean, and in terms of gaining competence in making new things. Several of the most common perspectives are

Art as process: compilation, integration, and synthesis of medium; technical, historical, and analytical knowledge and skills; inspiration and aspiration; and ideas that result in a work of art.

Art as product: involvement with completed works presented, performed, or available for study from various perspectives; and the multiple interrelationships and influences of completed work.

Art as an educative force: development of knowledge and skills in the arts, including mental and physical discipline gained from the study of art as process; and historical-cultural understanding gained from the study of completed work.

Art as communication: use of arts media and techniques to convey ideas and information for various purposes.

Art as a psychological phenomenon: the impact of arts media on human behavior.

Art as a physiological phenomenon: the impact of arts media on the human body.

Art as therapeutics: applications ranging from entertainment to psychology and psychiatry.

Art as social expression: correlations of artistic modes, products, and perceptions with specific groups.

Art as heritage: correlations of artistic activity with cultures and times.

Art as subject matter for other disciplines: use of points of view, methodologies, and contexts of the humanities, sciences, and social sciences to consider the impacts of art processes and products on intellectual, social, political, and other developments.

Intensive work involving these and other perspectives can be found throughout higher education. However, combinations, patterns, and emphases vary widely as various perspectives are mixed and balanced to achieve the goals and objectives of specific courses, curricula, and institutions, and in the work of specific faculty members.

Invention and Authenticity. Creative accomplishment as an artist means generating something that did not exist before. This is true whether the work is new, derivative, or interpretive. However, both newness and uniqueness are relative. While newness and uniqueness in and of themselves may be valid goals, much art making involves work within aesthetic, temporal, or spatial limits. These may be determined by the artist; conditions for use; the specifics and structures of choreography, scores, and scripts; the availability of resources; the wishes of clients; intellectual climates; available technologies; and so forth. Authentic work by artist faculty thus ranges from experimentation that produces radical departures to applications of originality in a variety of standard formats.

Simplicity and Complexity. Faculty in all disciplines are expected to work as experts with complex issues and problems. Although artist faculty are no exception, a perceptual difficulty must be noted: The complexities of a work of art may not be readily apparent. The immediate impression may be one of naturalness and simplicity, but this effect is achieved through complex techniques and structures that synthesize, integrate, and order multiple aesthetic elements.

Studying art is usually quite different. Often, the goal is to reveal the complexity of how things work, what happened and to what effect, and how meaning is evolving. Those considering the work of arts faculties in higher education need to understand these multiple approaches to complexity. Surface simplicity can produce illusions that deny the presence of background complexity. While surface simplicity can produce immediate appeal—the music of Mozart, for example—it is the background complexities that provide the substance for intellectual analysis from an artistic perspective. When dealing comprehensively with matters of art, it is essential to remember that tremendous intellectual effort is involved both in hiding complexity and revealing it. Two further points are essential. First, simplicity per se (without underlying complexity) is a valid and laudable aesthetic goal, especially in certain artistic styles. Second, scholarly analysis that uncovers simple principles guiding either complex or simple artworks can have all the attributes of analysis that uncovers underlying complexities.

Collaboration. Most visible in the performing arts, collaboration is present and growing in all arts disciplines. In collaborative situations, the individual artist's work is an essential part of an integrated whole. Collaboration thus occurs in conception, planning, and execution of a complete work. In this process, artists functioning singly and in groups regularly draw on knowledge and expertise from the sciences, humanities, and social sciences.

Collaboration is also increasing across the arts and other disciplines in teaching, research, and scholarship. Multi- and interdisciplinary work is a common goal. These collaborations regularly occur as arts-related issues are pursued within and among the various perspectives outlined previously.

Since collaboration requires compromise, approaches, new processes, and ways of thinking are regularly discovered. Collaboration thus energizes artistic and intellectual development.

Professional and Public Review. It is essential for faculty to place their work before professional communities and the public; however, those who make art may "publish" in formats quite different from those who study art and its impact. Although each institution will create its own definitions for evaluative and other purposes, performance, presentation, or installation of works of art serve the same function for those who work *in* art as publication in article or book form serves for those who do work *about* art.

Priorities. Each institution and academic unit concerned with the arts establishes priorities on many levels. Fundamental priorities are developed about the extent to which the arts will be present and what emphases will be given to specific arts. Within disciplines, some institutions focus on preparing artists; others, on preparing scholars; still others, on preparing teachers; some do all three and more.

Priorities are also established regarding the scope of disciplinary coverage. These decisions regularly control which elements of a discipline and its subdisciplines are means and which are ends in specific curricula. For example, the study of drawing can have a different relationship to the work of the prospective painter than to the work of the prospective designer or landscape architect.

Relationships between studies and activities associated with making, studying, and teaching art are also profoundly affected by decisions about scope and focus. Since priorities are directly related to mission, goals, and objectives, they constitute one framework for decisions concerning the work of the faculty.

Faculty Responsibilities. Within the context provided by mission, goals, objectives, and priorities, faculties undertake specific responsibilities. These involve particular focuses and interrelationships regarding (1) teaching that enables students to gain abilities with the media, processes, techniques, histories, and interdisciplinary relationships that comprise work in the arts disciplines, and to develop creative insight and critical judgment in aesthetic decision making; (2) creative work and research associated with making new things, discovering how things work, understanding what happened, and revealing what things mean; and (3) service that brings expertise to the work of the institution, the profession, and the larger community. In teaching, creative work, research, and service, art may be approached from single or multiple perspectives: process, product, educative force, communication, psychological phenomenon, physiological phenomenon, therapeutics, social expression, heritage, multidisciplinary, and so forth.

Some faculty members focus their efforts on an exclusive area of specialization; however, many faculty cover more than one area. Whatever the degree of specialization, or the content involved, all faculty work, including preparations for teaching and service, can utilize the processes of creation, discovery, analysis, integration, synthesis, application, and evaluation common to all intellectually based activity.

Arts faculty are regularly involved with one-on-one instruction where evaluation is constant from moment to moment as a work or presentation is made. Fulfilling this responsibility requires the ability to motivate, challenge, support, and direct individual students.

In practice, each faculty member has a specific profile of responsibilities showing relationships among such factors as competence, teaching assignments, area of creative or scholarly expertise, and philosophy about the role and purpose of the discipline. This profile may change constantly due to such influences as professional growth and institutional development. Interactions among these factors create the individual faculty member's approach to teaching, creative work and research, and service. Individual approaches are also deeply influenced by the nature of the field, the nature of traditions surrounding the field, and the nature of real or perceived expectations within the institution.

The above considerations demonstrate the infinite possibilities for developing sets of specific faculty responsibilities and expectations. For example, preparation of professionals in the arts disciplines requires teaching and learning about making new things, discovering how things work, understanding what happened, and revealing what things mean. Each faculty member will contribute by fulfilling a different set of responsibilities with respect to these activities. Thus, policies regarding faculties in the arts disciplines cannot be one-dimensional unless goals and objectives are centered around only one highly specialized activity. Determinations and evaluations of faculty responsibilities must be crafted according to the number of dimensions within the discipline covered by goals and objectives. These determinations and evaluations include attention to the elements, responsibilities, and perspectives previously covered.

Evaluation Issues. The task force addressed the following areas:

Defining Responsibilities. Effective and fair evaluation is based on clear and accurate statements regarding responsibilities and expectations. Such statements are critical because evaluations made by colleagues in the discipline, by students, by the institution, and by the individual faculty member can be quite different. For example, magnificent teaching as recognized by students may not carry significant weight with colleagues or with the institution. It is also important to be clear about the weight given various duties and perspectives—art as process, product, educative force, and so forth. This is particularly important when faculty members undertake vital responsibilities in the less glamorous or visible aspects of the profession. If a particular faculty responsibility is essential to the viability of the discipline, to development of students' fundamental competencies, and to the credibility of an institution's curriculum, then fulfillment of that responsibility should be judged on the basis of its importance rather than its stereotyped image.

Dealing with Complexity. If creation of new work and discovery of new knowledge are critical to the mission of an institution, evaluation mechanisms must have the capability to deal with various complex juxtapositions of perspective, technical competence, and inspiration that appear as these goals are pursued in the arts disciplines. The evaluation process must be able to deal with the objective and subjective natures of the arts. It must also account for the various imperatives involved in making art, in studying art, in studying the impact of art, and the interrelationship of all three. It must be able to deal with this interrelationship without pretending that one component is a substitute for another. It must be able to work with the arts on their own terms, and with the arts in terms appropriate to the humanities, the sciences, and the social sciences.

Determining Merit. Evaluation processes yield judgments about merit. Merit can be self-defined or defined in relation to other things. As important as intrinsic, extrinsic, and other perceptions are, it is also essential to consider merit in terms of goals, objectives, priorities, and mission. All such considerations may proceed from the perspective of the institution and the arts unit, or they may proceed from the perspectives of the discipline, of students, or of the individual faculty member. In any case, the particular arrangement of elements and perspectives used to determine merit must be considered and articulated as clearly as possible, especially at the time of faculty appointment.

Rewarding Teaching. Values concerning the role and purpose of teaching in cultural development are critical in every field. The teaching-cultural development connection has particular impact on the arts because work in the arts disciplines profoundly influence the cultural context that envelops and influences decisions and events. Since all work in the arts disciplines has multiple connections with education and cultural formation, teaching assumes particular importance. Evaluation policies and procedures should account for this fact so central to the nature and function of the arts within academe and in society as a whole.

Providing Opportunities. Institutions provide significant support to the work of arts faculty. However, the nature, scope, and availability of creative and research opportunities must be factors in considering productivity within a discipline. For example, the disparity between external research funding available to the arts and humanities in comparison to the sciences is beyond the control of institutions, academic units, or faculty members. Disparities can also occur with respect to release time and to opportunities for peer review when work cannot be distributed and studied in print form.

Focusing on Work. Modern public relations techniques make it possible to substitute notoriety for achievement, to confuse source or place with quality, and to confuse technical production features with content. Association with images of achievement is not achievement in and of itself. Images of quality are not a substitute for quality. Important work in the arts is not always immediately appreciated. Concepts such as national recognition need to be defined and used with care, since meaning may vary among disciplines, subdisciplines, institutions, and academic units.

Considering Innovation. Evaluative dilemmas can arise when disproportionate emphasis is placed on innovation, especially on innovation for its own sake. These dilemmas are particularly evident in the arts, where the most sophisticated evaluations cannot be based on empirical criteria, and where there is often no basis for comparison. It can be difficult to distinguish between genuine and apparent innovation, between new knowledge and new jargon, between fad initiation and aesthetic advancement. Multiple expert perspectives are useful in making these distinctions, but evaluation systems should avoid superficial use of the term *innovation.* They should also avoid attempts to use a common definition of innovation across the arts, sciences, humanities, and social sciences.

Working with Equivalencies. The complexity of issues involved in the work of faculty obviates the possibility of establishing exact equivalencies across academic disciplines. Policies designed to address equivalency should be consistent with the natures of the disciplines involved *and* with the mission, goals, and objectives of the institution. Methods can be devised to promote fairness. But no method in and of itself can produce empirical equivalence and ensure both fairness and a quality result at the same time.

Equivalencies are particularly difficult to formulate between work *in* and work *about* the arts disciplines. The challenge is to produce a reasonable policy based on specific goals and objectives while avoiding using one set of criteria as a template for the other.

Monitoring Technique. Overemphasis on specific assessment techniques can produce conditions where both work and evaluation are considered only in terms of what favored technologies and techniques can do. Work and evaluation having no mathematical base, or foreign to the techniques of a particular assessment, can be discounted. Goals and objectives fundamental to the work of a discipline or an academic unit can go unfulfilled or be lost altogether. Balancing technological means and technological thinking with other intellectual approaches is essential to effective evaluation of arts faculties.

Honoring Expertise. Each decision maker in higher education has values concerning the work of faculty derived from his or her own discipline and from perspectives gained by observing work in other disciplines. Although decision makers are required to make judgments that affect areas outside their disciplinary expertise, policies, evaluation methodologies, and protocols go only so far. There can be no substitute for the expertise of individuals within a discipline. Local efforts to define and reward the work of the faculty should place fundamental reliance on discipline-based expertise.

The members of the Interdisciplinary Task Force are *co-chairs*: Donald M. Lantzy, dean, College of Visual and Performing Arts, Syracuse University; Bruce Abbey, dean, School of Architecture, Syracuse University; *architecture*: Robert M. Beckley, FAIA, dean, College of Architecture, University of Michigan; Marvin Malecha, AIA, dean, College of Environmental Design, California State Polytechnic University; *art and design*: Robert Arnold, associate provost for curriculum and instruction, Ohio State University; Larry Walker, director, School of Art and Design, Georgia State University; *dance*: Nancy Smith Fichter, chair, Department of Dance, Florida State University; Ann Wagner, chair, Department of Dance, Saint Olaf College; *film and video*: Ben Levin, Department of Radio, Television, and Film, University of North Texas; *landscape architecture*: Sally Schauman, FASLA, chair, Department of Landscape Architecture, University of Washington; Mark Lindhult, ASLA, Department of Landscape Architecture, University of Massachusetts; *music*: Marilyn Taft Thomas, head, Department of Music, Carnegie-Mellon University; Kenneth A. Keeling, head, Department of Music, University of Tennessee; *theater*: James L. Steffensen, chair, Department of Drama, Dartmouth College; Carole W. Singleton, chair, Department of Drama, Howard University; *staff*: Samuel Hope, executive director, National Office for Arts Accreditation in Higher Education; John M. Maudlin-Jeronimo, executive director, National Architectural Accrediting Board; Karen P. Moynahan, associate director, National Office for Arts Accreditation in Higher Education; Karen L. Niles, staff vice president, planning and programs, Landscape Architecture Accrediting Board; Catherine Sentman, projects director, National Office for Arts Accreditation in Higher Education.

Faculty Work in Chemistry

Following is the *Report of the Task Force on the Definition of Scholarship in Chemistry* (American Chemical Society Task Force on the Definition of Scholarship in Chemistry, 1993) in its entirety:

This report is the result of deliberations of a special task force of the American Chemical Society to consider the definition of scholarship in the discipline of chemistry. The task force is part of a larger project being conducted by Syracuse University with grants from the Lilly Endowment and the Fund for the Improvement of Postsecondary Education. The goal of the Syracuse project, being carried out at a time of much change and questioning in higher education, is to develop a wide range of discipline-specific definitions of scholarship and scholarly work. The traditional way of categorizing and evaluating faculty activity in most of higher education has been in terms of teaching, research, and service. In the decades since World War II, research has come to occupy an elevated position in the major universities and to some degree throughout higher education. The elevated status of research has emerged due to its strong integral and interactive benefits in the development of chemists and chemistry (*vide infra*); however, this emphasis has become excessive in many institutions. Currently, many voices argue that the teaching of undergraduate students especially has suffered from this imbalance. The members of the task force agree that a wider and more flexible definition of scholarship is needed in chemistry. We propose such a reformulation.

Current Definition of Scholarship. For the past several decades the paradigm for scholarship in chemistry has been research. The words *scholarship* and *research* have become nearly synonymous in referring to the discovery of new knowledge about molecules and chemical systems; the publication of research papers, reviews, and monographs; the writing of grant proposals; the management of funded research projects; the contribution to scientific meetings; and the training of graduate students and postdoctoral associates. Faculty activities in the areas of undergraduate teaching and service, particularly at research universities, have been regarded as necessary and sometimes important but of a distinctly lower stature.

While the emphasis on research has contributed to high standards achieved by chemistry departments in the United States, this emphasis is inconsistent with the conditions presently confronting institutions of higher education, as well as the discipline of chemistry. Today, chemistry departments are faced, more than ever, with accountability to state legislatures that fund public institutions, to students and their parents who pay high tuition fees, and to the general public, who do not understand the science of chemistry or what happens in institutions of higher education. Furthermore, articulation with the precollege (K–12) educational system must be strengthened, and the level of scientific and technological literacy in the nation must be raised.

Within chemistry, the current definition of scholarship has led to faculty dissatisfaction, low morale, and lost potential. The headlong pursuit of research excellence has been accompanied by devaluation of the work of faculty members who are not very productive in research but who otherwise make important contributions. In many cases, these faculty members have had little motivation to contribute strongly to the overall activity of the department. In these changing times, these underutilized faculty members are an important resource for carrying out projects of importance to the department, such as curriculum revision or public outreach.

Generalized Scholarship. In order to provide a basis for responding to the changing needs of chemistry as a discipline, we offer a definition of scholarship in chemistry that is broader than the current definition. The new definition extends the range of recognized scholarship beyond traditional research. This definition recognizes that scholarship is an activity that can occur in many different forms and in a variety of areas. Scholarship can be viewed as an integrated process of reasoning, reflection, and communication that leads to new knowledge, insights, methods, or modes of thought. For a particular discipline, such as chemistry, there are many products of scholarship, as well as degrees of scholarship in various kinds of activities.

By extending the definition of scholarship beyond the area of research, the task force does not intend to diminish the importance of research to the discipline of chemistry. Rather, we seek to encourage individuals to carry out scholarship in other areas besides research and thereby contribute to the development, the learning, and the public presentation of chemistry. This encouragement will become tangible when individuals, from faculty members to the highest-level administrators, recognize and reward forms of chemistry scholarship other than research.

The general definition that we recommend describes scholarship in two dimensions. Along one dimension are four different areas of activity within which a number of elements can be found. These four areas are listed below without distinguishing relative importance. Likewise, the characteristic elements in each area are listed in no particular order and are intended to be illustrative. It is left to the institutions, departments, or organizational units that implement this definition to specify the relative importance to be placed on the four areas. In this way the definition is flexible and adaptable to various institutional settings in which scholarship in chemistry occurs, including the range of academic institutions from community colleges to research universities.

Scholarship Areas

Research	*Application*
Discovery	Industrial interactions
Integration	Implementation of new principles
Publications	Consulting

Research (continued)
   Grants
   Monographs

Teaching
   Classroom preparation
   Curriculum development
   Graduate student training
     and education
   Textbooks
   Multimedia materials

Application (continued)
   Technology transfer

Outreach
   Scientific literacy
   K–12 enrichment
   Extension service
   Ethics
   Minority and gender-based
     recruitment and retention

The second dimension of the generalized definition of scholarship is a set of criteria, each of which may vary along a continuum from the highest degree to the lowest degree for the evaluation of the quality or degree of scholarship in any of the four scholarship areas along the first dimension. For a given area, or a specific activity in that area, the importance of the scholarship can be evaluated along the second dimension using the criteria in the following list: degree or extent of (1) peer-reviewed publications (journal articles, books or monographs), (2) recognition by colleagues and organizations (invited papers and colloquia, awards), (3) financial support (competitive peer-reviewed grants, industrial or home-institutional support).

At the highest level of scholarship in a given area, there is publication in the most respected journals, fame and international recognition, and substantial grant support. At the lowest level there is no communication with peers, no recognition outside the immediate activity, and no financial support. It is possible to reach the highest level of scholarship in any of the four areas listed, although it is most common to do so in the area of research. The task force recognizes the fact that mechanisms for gauging scholarship outside of research are not generally or firmly in place. We encourage the creative development of new approaches to measure scholarship in chemistry across a broad spectrum of activities.

Throughout this report, colleges and universities are the specific context for which the general definition of scholarship is discussed, and the particular issues faced by industry and government laboratories are not addressed. Nevertheless, the task force believes that the definition of generalized scholarship given below can be modified for use outside of higher education by a suitable weighting or augmentation of the areas of scholarship listed.

The task force feels that research enjoys a unique status relative to the other three areas: application, teaching, and outreach. Of these areas, research is the only one that consists entirely of scholarship. One cannot carry out research without being involved in scholarly activity. On the other hand, for the other areas, there is often a significant component of the activity that is not scholarship. These nonscholarship components are usually activities that are supported by or promote scholarship and are vital to the sustenance of excellence.

In choosing the areas in which scholarship occurs, we have been influenced by the writings of Ernest Boyer and others who subdivide forms of scholarship into the scholarship of discovery, the scholarship of integration, the scholarship of application, and the scholarship of teaching. In adapting this framework to the discipline of chemistry, we have combined the scholarships of discovery and integration of knowledge into research, and we have added an area that we refer to as the scholarship of outreach.

For illustrative purposes we present a few examples of scholarship outside the area of research. In the case of teaching, scholarship can take the form of writing a textbook that contains a fresh, innovative outlook or a reasoned, alternative organization of the subject material. Scholarship may involve developing a new course for nonspecialists, approaches to teaching chemical concepts, or developing new experiments or novel lecture demonstrations. In the examples of curriculum development, an important component of the scholarly activity is the publication or the dissemination of the results of the development. Similarly, in the case of community outreach, new approaches to arousing the interest of elementary school children in science, to stimulating high school students to study science, and to communicating such insights through books, monographs, reports, or other publications represents an important form of scholarship. Interest in outreach is an area of vital importance to the discipline of chemistry that is relatively undeveloped. In this area the number of avenues available for the expression of scholarship is more limited than for research, but more opportunities should arise in the future. In particular, it is important that chemistry faculty find ways to heighten the public understanding of science, for example, by making contributions to courses in scientific literacy.

Although the definition of scholarship adopted by the task force is general, there are several areas associated with scholarship in chemistry (and, more generally, the sciences) that are discipline-specific. One is the considerable expense of carrying out research at the highest levels of excellence and innovation. Only a relatively select group of institutions have the financial resources to maintain first-rate research chemistry faculty and research programs. Another area is the close relation between teaching and research discussed in some detail above. In chemistry, as well as in other scientific fields, there is a very close symbiotic relationship between graduate student and mentor that simultaneously involves a teaching and a research function. Such relationships are also found in the best undergraduate instruction. Because the field of chemistry evolves rapidly, accurate and relevant instruction in this subject, even at the introductory level, requires teachers in tune with current developments in chemistry and teachers who appreciate the nature of research in chemistry. An additional problem that arises for teachers of introductory chemistry is making wise choices of what to teach.

Importance of Scholarship. Scholarship represents the highest level of intellectual activity in the various areas of chemistry. It corresponds to those elements of activity that are new, thought-provoking, interactive, long-lasting and transportable between individuals or organizational units. Scholarship at the highest levels is what all strive to achieve.

The task force believes that involvement in research in the discipline currently or during one's formal education is necessary to achieve excellence in performance and high levels of scholarship in the other areas outlined above. Thus, a Ph.D. remains the proper preparation. This is particularly true for the area of teaching. It is often observed that outstanding teachers are active and enthusiastic researchers. There is a strong interplay between teaching and research, which is vital to the former. Chemistry is a discipline where discoveries and new concepts of a fundamental nature are continually occurring. To stay current as a teacher and to appreciate the limits of established principles, a teacher must have had direct experience with the research process and the scientific method. Outstanding teachers reach beyond the bounds of standard textbook material in a scholarly manner to expose students to new developments in chemistry.

An impression that the task force does not intend is that activities that do not fall into the category of scholarship are not important. There are many activities in the areas of application, teaching, and research that will be on the border between scholarship and nonscholarship, between the reasoned, reflective activity leading to communication of methods and ideas to others and the simple act of working out the details of an application, grading examination questions, gathering information, or performing some forms of outreach activity. All of these activities are important to the overall mission of chemistry. It is far less important to worry about what things are called than it is to recognize and nurture important activities. An organizational unit should find ways to encourage a wider range of individual contribution so that the goals of that unit can be approached more rapidly and effectively. Yet, it should be kept in mind that scholarship, in the broad sense, is the heart of all faculty activities, and a continual commitment to scholarship underlies and sustains excellence in these activities.

Conclusion. The fundamental conclusion of this report is that scholarship takes place in a wide variety of activities related to the discipline of chemistry. We have provided a framework for identifying and evaluating the significance of these various forms of scholarship. Within this framework, we conclude that although research is only scholarship, not all scholarship is research. We believe that the traditional division of faculty performance into the categories of teaching, research, and service is still useful and valid, provided that it is recognized that scholarship can also occur in the areas of teaching and service.

In this report we have recommended an extension of the current definition of scholarship in chemistry. The new definition is general and can be adapted to a wide range of organizational units in academics, industry, or government by specifying the relative importance of the various areas presented, or even adding new ones as desired. The report stresses the importance of scholarship in chemistry but also recognizes the importance of nonscholarship activities that are directly or indirectly supportive of and supported by scholarship. It hoped that the expanded definition of scholarship will foster a more complete and efficient involvement of individuals in organizational units, an involvement in which a wider range of talents is brought to bear on important issues to chemistry in these times of change, growth, and adaptation.

The members of the American Chemical Society Task Force on the Definition of Scholarship in Chemistry are: William E. Broderick, State University of New York, Albany; Paula P. Brownlee, Association of American Colleges; Norman C. Craig, Oberlin College; Marcetta Y. Darensbourg, Texas A&M University; William B. DeLauder, Delaware State College; Slayton A. Evans, Jr., University of North Carolina; J. Ivan Legg, Memphis State University (co-chair); Ursula M. Mazur, Washington State University; Edward K. Mellon, Florida State University; Joseph G. Morse, Utah State University; Laurence A. Nafie, Syracuse University (co-chair); and Theodore E. Tabor, Dow Chemical Company.

Faculty Work in Geography

Following is *Toward a Reconsideration of Faculty Roles and Rewards in Geography* (Association of American Geographers [AAG] Special Committee on Faculty Roles and Rewards, 1993) in its entirety:

Faculty Roles and Rewards. Geographers employed in American colleges and universities have for too long been hired to do one job and rewarded for doing another. Members of the professoriate have been engaged to teach, but earning tenure, promotion and salary increases have hinged primarily on research productivity. Until the 1970s, granting promotion and tenure was often the unreviewed prerogative of deans and other administrative officers. Salary increases were often determined solely by department chairs or heads. Many American academic institutions moved to formalize reward procedures in the 1970s and 1980s. As schemes for allocating awards became more bureaucratized, teaching, research, and service emerged as a trinity of faculty roles that was examined to determine whether candidates should be awarded promotion, tenure, and, in some instances, merit pay increases.

Evaluation of these roles differs in rigor and detail. Assessments of teaching customarily have focused on formal classroom instruction and graduate supervision. Evidence of teaching accomplishments consists of student evaluations supplemented by occasional peer reviews. In the sciences, research is typically equated with publication, and peer-reviewed journal articles are accorded the highest status. The humanities look for books and monographs as evidence of proficiency, whereas public performance or shows are viewed as marks of excellence in the fine arts and effective practice is respected in the professions. Service is a catchall for laudable activities that are neither teaching nor research. Often, it is assayed by counting the number of performances given, offices held, and responsibilities discharged, but verification of the quality and the outcomes of service contributions is rare. Research usually outweighs other roles in faculty reward formulas. Teaching and service are accorded less value, often to the point that they are not subjected to the kind of peer review inherent to measures of research productivity.

Neither American faculty members nor the American public seem satisfied with the priorities explicit and implicit in existing faculty reward schemes. Several comprehensive surveys reveal that professors across the spectrum of American colleges and universities question the weights currently attached to faculty roles; they prefer more balance among the three categories and more rewards for good teaching. Society demands much of its colleges and universities, but above all it asks that they be places where undergraduate teaching is an important mission. Many people sacrifice a great deal to send their children or themselves to college, and they—and the legislators who represent them in supporting public higher education—expect faculty to be concerned, first, with good instruction. Both the consumers and the producers of higher education have expressed unambiguous discontent over priorities of late, and in the last few years criticism has become sharp, and even strident.

A consequence of the criticism as well as a catalyst for reconsidering faculty roles and rewards was Ernest Boyer's (1990) report for the Carnegie Foundation titled *Scholarship Reconsidered: Priorities for the Professoriate.* Boyer proposed to break out of the "tired old teaching versus research debate" by reaffirming the values of teaching and service. He adopted Eugene Rice's four categories of scholarship: discovery, integration, application, and teaching. Although Boyer's four kinds of scholarship offer useful springboards for rethinking faculty roles, they do not match pervasive terminology, and they engender surprisingly vociferous disagreements among different disciplines about the nature of scholarship.

As traditionally used, the word *research* necessarily includes Rice's scholarship of discovery—the pursuit and creation of knowledge. But geographers commonly designate as research what Boyer calls the scholarship of integration. For geographers, integrative work may mean melding discoveries in their own discipline with those from other specialties to create larger systems of meaning. That integration may be an end in itself, as in a monograph describing a place or a region; it may be a prelude to addressing a topical problem from a geographical perspective. Those who profess some subfields of geography will distinguish integrative and interpretive work from the research of discovery, while others, in other geographic specialties, will view that distinction as trivial or even specious.

Boyer defines the scholarship of application as responsibly applying knowledge to consequential problems. Geographers could interpret that definition in ways ranging from choosing basic research topics that have social and environmental significance, to engaging in routine problem solving for a public agency or private corporation.

Boyer's scholarship of teaching relies on building bridges between an instructor's understanding and a student's learning, and in that process transforming and extending knowledge. The concept is apt for geography, but conventional usage of the word *student* evokes images of campus-situated, tuition-paying, degree-seeking young adults. Geographers also offer workshops for practitioners, seminars for policymakers, guest presentations in junior high school classes, and other extramural instruction. The Boyer and Rice four-part scheme is a starting point for reconceptualizing faculty roles, but it stretches customary terminology too far to be widely adopted.

Roles and Rewards in Geography. We favor four roles that focus on the content of faculty activities in geography. We recognize that each institution has its own ways of defining faculty roles, some open and fluid, some highly circumscribed. In translating the terms we use, each geography program will need to adapt the concepts presented below to the missions and nomenclatures prevalent in local evaluation and reward procedures. Where objectives and the ways faculty rewards are tied to them have not been articulated, that task should be given high priority.

Teaching. For the immediate future, classroom and laboratory instruction and thesis advising will continue to be central components of the teaching role. Professing geographers are employed by colleges and universities devoted to classroom instruction. Therefore, they will continue to draw on their general knowledge of the discipline and appropriate lessons from their personal research to acquaint students in their introductory courses with how the world works geographically. They will use a different blend of general and personal perspectives to lead undergraduate majors and graduate students to progressively deeper understandings of the discipline, its links with other specialties, and its place in society. More often than not, these encounters will occur in traditional settings of classes, seminars, and thesis tutorials. For these teaching roles, traditional reward mechanisms, appropriately rebalanced, may suffice.

Yet teaching has many diverse facets in all kinds of academic institutions.

Some of these dimensions are common to most disciplines; they include

Advising undergraduates to design degree programs and evaluate career
    options
Advising undergraduate senior research papers
Conceiving and implementing new courses and curricula
Developing and experimenting with innovative teaching approaches
Designing and teaching in courses and programs that integrate geography
    with other disciplines
Initiating and participating in cooperative curriculum programs with other
    institutions
Establishing and supervising student internships
Adapting computer equipment and software to curriculum needs and
    integrating computer-assisted instruction into curricula.

Some that are particularly important in geography are

Preparing for and serving in foreign studies programs
Instructing K–12 teachers (especially important in geography because,
    until recently, virtually no students entered college or university
    intending to major in geography, and because of the emphasis on
    upgrading secondary school geography in the 1990s)
Preparing for and conducting frequent and extended field trips
Winning funding for the specialized computer equipment that is increas-
    ingly prerequisite to responsible instruction in geography, and then
    setting up and maintaining the laboratories containing that equipment
Teaching cartography, which demands far more time per student than
    most courses because it can be taught well only tutorially.

Teaching geography involves instructing audiences well beyond traditional, intramural, tuition-paying students. Geographers often find their
expertise sought outside campus boundaries in venues that impose special
demands of time and intellectual commitment that should be recognized in
faculty evaluation and reward schemes. Faculty increasingly are called on to
convey information and decision-making approaches to the larger communities that provide their students and support for their institutions. The range
of such teaching opportunities will be elaborated on later in the section on
outreach.

Faculty, academic officers, and those who pay the bills for higher
education will all be more satisfied with faculty reward outcomes if all
teaching roles are subjected to peer review. Restricting the reward system
purview to traditional classroom and thesis advising responsibilities would
be shortsighted, particularly in light of the opportunities for innovative,
computer-based self-instruction that will emerge in the next decade.

Research. Research in geography encompasses three forms of creative work:

1. Geographers engaged in *basic* research hope to produce or discover new knowledge about the world we inhabit and the ways it functions. In that effort, geographers use an unusual number of conceptual and analytical approaches, ranging from those of the earth sciences to those of the humanities. We include in our definition of basic research in geography attempts to enhance the distinctive methods geographers use in their work, such as cartography, geographical information system, remote sensing, and spatial statistics.

2. Geographers who pursue *synthesizing* research seek to combine basic research findings from across the remarkably large number of subfields within the discipline, integrate results from cognate disciplines into geographical analysis and theory, and merge existing and new knowledge about a place or region into a cohesive portrayal of a place or region, either as an entity of intrinsic interest or as the locus of a topical phenomenon or problem.

3. Academic geographers engaged in *applied* research (as distinct from geographers who *practice* in the private and public sectors) focus on solving "practical" problems. They may pose the issues they address, or they may respond to challenges arising in relevant agencies, firms, or industries. Although geographers who prefer applied research often apply the results of basic research to extramural problems, ideas flow in both directions between basic and applied research. Basic questions often arise in the course of trying to solve a seemingly straightforward practical problem.

As noted earlier, geographers who can demonstrate proficiency in basic research have an inside track in winning professional recognition and the tangible rewards that accompany it. Those who concentrate on synthesizing and applied research probably will have to work harder and longer for equivalent rewards, even though synthesizing and applied research have been firmly embedded in the geographical research tradition.

Basic research will persist as a foundation for all other kinds of research in geography. Accordingly, geographers should continue to value it highly, evaluate its quality rigorously, and reward it appropriately. Nevertheless, that priority does not imply that basic research should continue to be accorded its traditional weight relative to synthesizing and applied research. Integration and application deserve greater returns than have customarily accrued to them. To achieve that rebalancing, the products of synthesis and application must be subjected to the same intensity of peer evaluation that is used to assess basic research.

Outreach. Service often has been used as a catchall category to encompass work not clearly included under the traditional rubrics of teaching and research. We think of a third role geographers play as outreach. Outreach in geography includes, among other activities, responding to requests to undertake applied research projects; consulting in the public and private sectors; helping improve geography instruction in primary, secondary, and postsecondary schools; explaining one's discipline or research using mass media; writing for lay audiences; testifying as an expert in legislative or judicial settings; lecturing to the public; and serving on boards and commissions that draw on and enhance disciplinary and professional expertise.

Geographers deal with the world as it exists and as it might be. They have much of great value to say about environmental and human problems across a spectrum of analytical scales ranging from localities to the globe. In lending their energies to those problems in ways that depend on and exercise their expertise, geographers fulfill a mandate implicit in the intellectual heritage they cultivate. Accordingly, outreach should be valued more highly than it has been in most academic institutions since World War II. Individual programs will accord outreach different weights when striking their own balances among faculty roles, but more incentives for faculty to undertake outreach would yield worthwhile dividends, including greater visibility resulting from the appreciation by decision makers and the public of contributions to the solution of societal problems, augmented theoretical development engendered by the propensity of the world to work contrary to theory-based expectations, enhanced faculty proficiency in both teaching and research as a result of grappling with substantive problems, laboratory and field experience for students, including internships, and increased financial support for students and equipment purchase based on better knowledge of agency and industry needs and funding opportunities.

Citizenship. Citizenship obligations accompany every professorial appointment. One way faculty members exercise citizenship is by service within their programs or departments. As the term implies, all faculty members take some share of common responsibilities. Within any program, tasks will be allocated as needed for the ongoing functioning of the organization. Citizenship at the institutional scale maintains a program's visibility on campus, and individual faculty members must assume an appropriate share of such corporate responsibilities. Occasionally, citizenship within an institution may draw on a faculty member's geographical expertise in the same way that local bodies may call on it. Occasionally, exceptionally large citizenship commitments may be required without significant work reduction, such as presiding over a faculty senate or chairing a major university task force. On such occasions, recognition beyond that accorded to expected levels of outreach should be given.

A second arena in which faculty members discharge citizenship responsibilities is their disciplines. Faculty reasonably can be expected to review journal manuscripts and research proposals, advise extramural colleagues on work in progress, write letters of recommendation for students and for colleagues, and accept appointments to the committees of scholarly societies. As with institutional citizenship, disciplinary service sometimes may require extraordinary commitments that warrant extraordinary recognition; an example would be serving as president of a scholarly society.

The fulfillment of civic responsibilities should not be confused with professorial citizenship. However laudable, an activity that is not grounded in disciplinary knowledge, faculty role expertise, or both has no place in faculty reward evaluations. Speaking about geography to your daughter's elementary school class during Geography Awareness Week may be an instance of outreach; speaking to your daughter's class on your hobby is not.

Overlap. Teaching, research, outreach, and citizenship comprise a fuzzy set; they overlap and intermingle. The settings in which faculty play the three roles often determine how geographers classify identical contributions. One program's applied research, for example, may be another institution's outreach. General definitions will remain arguable and imprecise, but each institution should have little difficulty formulating its own appropriate conceptualizations, assuming it has clearly articulated missions. Such imprecision and variation do not gainsay the validity of this or any other general schema or the roles they attempt to encapsulate. Roles and categories are both elements of a coherent process of discovering, refining, integrating, transmitting, and applying geographical knowledge. Teaching, research, and outreach and citizenship—whatever the fuzziness of their boundaries generally and locally—inform and enrich one another. They form a continuum of creative and pedagogical activities that differ less in content and mode than in the locations where they play out and in the clienteles they address.

Distinctive Roles and Rewards. A set of pressing current issues taps the expertise of geographers in ways that should be incorporated into their role and reward schemes. Opportunities and problems arising from the globalization of the world's economic systems, and from the linkages between global systems and local business and industry, are the stuff of contemporary economic geography. The study of global environments and their connections to human activities in locales and regions persists as the cornerstone of geographical research and teaching. As colleges and universities continue to reexamine and recast their curricula, geography's many ties with cognate disciplines provide special and challenging opportunities to contribute an integrated view to discussions among disciplinary specialists. In pedagogy, emphases on mapping, fieldwork, and laboratory demonstration augment the traditional formats of instruction in classrooms, libraries, and tutorials. Geographers already employ the diversity of learning modes on which expanded educational missions of the future will rely. Because of the breadth of perspectives they embrace, geographers are already experienced in what other specialties are beginning to attempt.

Recommendations. First, we recommend that competent teaching— verified by rigorous peer review—be a *necessary condition* of retention and advancement in all professorial positions in geography in all academic ·

institutions. Teaching should be valued more highly in allocating faculty rewards than it has been for the last several decades, especially in relation to discovery.

Disciplinary considerations aside, all students deserve faculty who are able teachers; ideally they should have access to talented and dedicated teachers. Teaching is an especially critical faculty role in geography programs for two reasons. First, the integrative and synthetic nature of geography demands clear and coherent exposition if it is to be conveyed properly, effectively received, and intelligently acted on by students, whatever the venue in which they are taught. Second, few students enter colleges and universities intending to major in geography. Almost every one of the more than three thousand U.S. students who earn baccalaureate degrees in geography every year was attracted to the discipline by an excellent teacher who offered compelling course content in an introductory course. Morality and disciplinary progress demand that good—not just adequate—instruction be a necessary condition of all professorial appointments. Geographers take society's coin for educating its citizens, and their specialty cannot thrive absent devotion to that role.

Teaching competence should be verified by rigorous peer review. A variety of measures should be used to assess teaching, including student evaluations, teaching portfolios, and classroom visits by peers. Academic administrators should seek from colleagues or administrators responsible for cross-disciplinary programs evidence of satisfactory and exceptional accomplishment for teaching conducted outside geography programs. We reiterate our recommendation that teaching be accorded higher value in promotion, tenure, salary, and other reward allocations than it has been given over the last several decades, especially in relation to research.

Second, we recommend that rigorously peer-reviewed research be accorded first priority in allocating faculty rewards in geography programs whose missions contain a major research component. Peer review of research should focus more than it currently does on the quality and originality of research publications as well as on their number. We further recommend that institutions be realistic about their emphasis on research in relation to other institutional demands on faculty time. A chancellor who presses faculty to conduct research in an institution with a five-course-per-semester teaching load has undertaken a fool's errand. The importance of the research component will continue to differ among institutions in higher education. Where research is not a primary mission element, the performance of teaching or outreach roles should outweigh research in importance in the allocation of faculty rewards.

Even in institutions and programs whose mission is principally or indeed exclusively instructional, teaching, as scholarly work, should be informed by active research. To profess geography should mean to participate in the ongoing elaboration of knowledge in the discipline. To profess geography is to go beyond being a passive conduit for insights borrowed from others. To profess is to spark in students the capacity for independent learning that is best stimulated by personal engagement, however limited, in original research. Teaching unalloyed with at least some research risks leaving students with only the content of geography, and denying them insight into the processes that create that content. We recognize the obstacles to research that confront colleagues in programs with crushing teaching loads. Those obstacles should challenge the entire discipline to convince the leaders of teaching institutions of the shortsightedness of denying their faculty opportunities to engage in the research and outreach that can immeasurably enrich teaching.

Third, we recommend that outreach (the traditional service category) be carefully rethought to tease out its distinctively geographical components, and that consideration be given to the degree to which they overlap and complement teaching and research. Where outreach in its various guises forms a major component of program and institutional missions, it should be weighted proportionately in the faculty reward equation. We recommend that geography programs (1) examine their missions and arrive at consensus regarding the importance of outreach; (2) develop coherent, systematic plans for evaluating and valuing outreach roles; procedures should include peer as well as client evaluation of outreach results; and (3) ensure that the results of outreach roles feed back into teaching and basic research.

To serve as a basis for faculty rewards, outreach should be rooted in disciplinary expertise and it should be fertile. It should differ from routine consulting or practice by offering the potential for deepening a discipline's understanding and expanding the scope of its application. Faculty should be encouraged to disseminate the results of outreach roles in appropriate ways. When a stint of exceptionally demanding outreach warrants special consideration in the reward scheme, the work performed should be carefully reviewed by an external group of peers who engage in the same kind of work.

Fourth, we recommend that the discharge of normal citizenship responsibilities, whether intra- or extramural, not be deemed worthy of special notes in allocating rewards. Exceptional contributions deserve consideration appropriate to a program's missions. If institutional and disciplinary citizenship are terms entered into the reward equation, they should be evaluated formally (without becoming compulsive) rather than via the informal judgments of colleagues. Assessments of institutional and professional citizenship should be based on annual activity reports, letters of appreciation that go beyond the perfunctory thanks, and especially requests that an individual give repeat performances. (No good deed ever goes unpunished!) The absence of evidence of unsatisfactory citizenship should never be interpreted as satisfactory performance. Creative measures of the quality and quantity of such contributions would be helpful.

Fifth, we recommend that programs formulate mission statements to guide the setting of faculty roles and the allocation of rewards among those who perform them. Much of the stress over faculty roles and rewards emanates from the absence of clear mission statements that would provide a coherent framework for evaluating faculty performance. When such mission statements exist, they are often not linked to faculty roles and rewards in ways that are obvious to faculty members, especially junior scholars. Faculty members deserve unambiguous statements of the missions of the institutions and programs in which they profess. They deserve accurate descriptions of the criteria that will be used to assess how much they contribute to those missions. They deserve criteria that have been formulated in ways that permit them to document the quality and the quantity of those contributions.

Sixth, we recommend that definitions of faculty rewards be broadened beyond current formulations. Academic geographers earn external and internal rewards for fulfilling their roles well. External rewards may include job security in the form of long-term tenure; promotion to higher academic ranks; merit increases of base salaries; temporary salary augmentations; grants to underwrite research; reimbursement for expenses of fieldwork, travel, conference participation, and research materials; working space and equipment; student assistance; prizes and awards; and public and peer recognition.

Internal rewards may include personal satisfaction over role performance that yields an enhanced sense of self-worth and pride in accomplishment, unusual opportunities for self-reflection, freedom to redirect one's professional efforts, a high degree of professional autonomy, and abundant opportunities to contribute to community welfare by drawing on professional expertise. Faculty reward schemes in American colleges and universities focus primarily on external awards for good reason—it is easier to obtain and allocate external awards than to cultivate the leadership skills that arouse faculty members' internal motivations.

In an era when external rewards are likely to remain stagnant, it is worth reminding ourselves that great leaders usually offer their followers few external rewards. On the contrary, their followers often make great personal sacrifices to enlist in powerful movements because they have been convinced that they are engaging in a great cause that ennobles their lives. The pursuit, transformation, and transmission of knowledge is a great cause. Individual faculty members, caught up in the whirlwinds of the many jobs they do, easily forget about the larger enterprise in which they are engaged. Program and institutional leaders squander a powerful motivation and abdicate leadership responsibilities when they fail frequently to remind their faculty of the nobility of the roles they perform.

Finally, we recommend that academic administrators and faculty acknowledge that reward mechanisms are now based almost entirely on individualistic conceptions of faculty roles. Without exception in the committee's experience, rewards accrue to individuals evaluated in isolation. That view of faculty roles may prevail for some time. We opine, however, that the kinds of collaborative and team efforts that have proved productive in other industries eventually will prove useful in geography, probably in the form of instructional teams using several complementary methods of instruction. Research in geography also may move beyond the artisan or craft scale that currently prevails, to projects that are addressed collaboratively by organized groups.

Different individuals make different kinds of contributions to the success of a program. Excellent teaching and advising, outstanding research, intensive outreach, and heroic citizenship rarely are embodied in the same individuals. Therefore, the corporate success of most programs depends on individual faculty contributing more to some roles than to others. Reward systems that respond to that reality engender better relationships among colleagues and foster the achievement of collective program goals. We believe that thinking about ways to define roles and allocate rewards on a supra-individual basis deserves consideration as part of the general, long-term rethinking of reward schemes.

Recommendations Are Not Prescriptions. In preparing these recommendations, we debated a variety of ways of conceptualizing faculty roles and rewards, including those used across a spectrum of academic institutions. We drew on the customs, procedures, and practices used in determining faculty roles and rewards in specialties as different as chemistry and fine arts. We sought to cast these recommendations in a framework that is generic enough to be used, with local modifications, in almost any academic institution. We are confident that these recommendations are well founded in the experience and thinking of the wide range of institutions and disciplines we reviewed, but we stress the need to tailor their implementation to local expectations regarding faculty roles.

Institutional missions vary greatly among American colleges and universities, and program missions differ considerably, not only among institutions but also within them. A geography program in a university whose primary mission is research may choose to concentrate on teaching and outreach. Alternatively, a geography program in an avowedly teaching institution may develop exceptional research expertise, and the institution's officers may elect to protect and enhance that role for its intrinsic and extrinsic value. A role and reward structure that fails to accommodate such local conditions is unlikely to yield satisfying results.

These recommendations will be helpful only as they are tailored to what institutions and constituent units need to do and to the expertise and preferences of the faculty members who must meet those needs. Specificity in applying these recommendations should be carried well beyond program levels. Negotiated modifications of these general principles that suit individual faculty members, and indeed the several stages that occur in an individual's career cycle, should be expected and welcome. Failure to seek and find appropriate specificity will increase the risk of substituting new and different mismatches between faculty and institutional expectations for the traditional mismatches we hope to remedy.

The members of the AAG Special Committee on Faculty Roles and Rewards are John S. Adams, University of Minnesota (co-chair); Susan Brooker-Gross, Virginia Polytechnic Institute; Laura Conkey, Dartmouth College; Edward Fernald, Florida State University; Ernst Griffin, San Diego State University; John Mercer, Syracuse University (co-chair); Norman Moline, Augustana College; and Ronald Abler, AAG (ex officio).

References

American Assembly of Collegiate Schools of Business. *Standards for Accreditation in Accounting and Business*. St. Louis: American Assembly of Collegiate Schools of Business, 1991.

American Assembly of Collegiate Schools of Business Task Force on Faculty Research. *Final Report of the Task Force on Faculty Research*. St. Louis: American Assembly of Collegiate Schools of Business, 1987.

American Chemical Society Task Force on the Definition of Scholarship in Chemistry. *Report of the Task Force on the Definition of Scholarship in Chemistry*. Washington, D.C.: American Chemical Society, 1993.

American Historical Association. *Statement on Standards of Professional Conduct*. Washington, D.C.: American Historical Association, 1992.

American Historical Association Ad Hoc Committee on Redefining Scholarly Work. *Redefining Historical Scholarship*. Washington, D.C.: American Historical Association, 1992.

American Historical Association Ad Hoc Committee on the Future of the AHA. *Report of the Ad Hoc Committee on the Future of the AHA*. Washington, D.C.: American Historical Association, 1988.

Association of American Geographers Special Committee on Faculty Roles and Rewards. *Toward a Reconsideration of Faculty Roles and Rewards in Geography*. San Antonio, Tex.: Association of American Geographers, 1993.

Boyer, E. L. *Scholarship Reconsidered: Priorities for the Professoriate*. Princeton, N.J.: Carnegie Foundation for the Advancement of Teaching, 1990.

Interdisciplinary Task Force. *The Work of Arts Faculties in Higher Education*. Washington, D.C.: Interdisciplinary Task Force, 1992.

Laidlaw, W. K. *Defining Scholarly Work in Management Education*. St. Louis: American Assembly of Collegiate Schools of Business, 1992.

Lynton, E. "What Makes It Scholarly." Paper presented at the conference Redefinition and Assessment of Scholarship, Syracuse, New York, July 1992.

Porter, L., and McKibbin, L. *Management Education and Development: Drift or Thrust into the 21st Century?* New York: McGraw-Hill, 1988.

Rice, R. E. "The New American Scholar: Scholarship and the Purposes of the University." *Metropolitan Universities Journal,* 1991, *1* (4), 7–18.

Schlereth, T. J. "Museum Exhibition Reviews: Introduction." *Journal of American History,* June 1989, pp. 192–195.

BRONWYN E. ADAM is assistant project director at the Center for Instructional Development, Syracuse University.

ALTON O. ROBERTS is director of instructional design at the Center for Instructional Development, Syracuse University.

Changes in faculty roles and rewards are under way across the nation. How institutions approach change depends on their missions and campus cultures.

Institutional Approaches to the Issues of Reward and Scholarship

Alton O. Roberts, Jon F. Wergin, Bronwyn E. Adam

A growing number of institutions of higher education are working to address the interrelated issues of institutional mission, teaching quality, and faculty roles and rewards. In this chapter, we provide examples of these deliberations in the space available, recognizing that the nature and structure of an institution, the style of its administration, and the differences among the disciplines all play roles in determining how the process of change is approached on a given campus. While some colleges and universities have begun the dialogue by focusing on enhancement of the undergraduate experience, others have used *Scholarship Reconsidered: Priorities for the Professoriate* (Boyer, 1990) as their starting point. Some campuses have begun this process in an interactive fashion, while others have used a more direct administrative approach. Despite these differences, the processes of change illustrated here share several characteristics. All depend on the active participation of faculty and administrators (developing ownership), a sensitivity to the specific nature of the individual campuses (knowing the context), and a sensitivity to the differences among the academic disciplines (recognizing loyalties).

First, we present sample documents, with minor adaptations, from three institutions, and a synthesis of documents from a fourth, that delineate institutional change from different perspectives. Next, we describe a process of change initiated by seven campuses working together. Finally, using a sample of an additional ten institutions, we briefly describe the initiatives that are under way and include the name of a campus contact person for each institution.

NEW DIRECTIONS FOR HIGHER EDUCATION, no. 81, Spring 1993   © Jossey-Bass Publishers

Improving the Climate for Teaching: University of Wisconsin, Madison

The University of Wisconsin at Madison, an urban institution and the state's flagship research university, consists of eleven schools and colleges with 2,325 faculty, 28,900 undergraduate students, and 14,296 graduate students.

As early as 1989, the vice chancellor for academic affairs, David Ward, charged the Committee on Undergraduate Education with the task of renewing emphasis on the quality of undergraduate education. Enhancement of undergraduate education continues to be a primary goal of the institution as evidenced by the report and recommendations prepared by Richard Barrows, associate vice chancellor for undergraduate education and student academic services (Barrows, 1993).

On another front, the Faculty Senate's University Committee formed the Committee on Teaching Quality, Evaluation, and Rewards late in 1991. The Executive Summary of their report, presented below, constitutes an especially complete and well-wrought rationale for the initiatives that they developed. Eight of the eleven recommendations were approved by the Faculty Senate in February 1993. Approval of the others is pending.

Following is the Executive Summary of the *Report of the Committee on Teaching Quality, Evaluation, and Rewards* (Committee on Teaching Quality, Evaluation, and Rewards, 1992):

The Committee on Teaching Quality, Evaluation, and Rewards was formed by the University Committee on December 6, 1991, to report to the Faculty Senate with recommendations to improve the quality, rewards, and incentives for teaching on the Madison campus. The scope was broad, and this report reflects that broad scope. The charge also reflects some of the concerns and recommendations of the 1989 Future Directions Committee.

Although this was a faculty committee that focused primarily on resident classroom instruction, there are aspects of the recommendations that apply to outreach forms of teaching and to the teaching accomplishments of the academic staff. We urge all faculty and staff to utilize as much of the material contained herein as is appropriate to stimulate discussion and to modify as appropriate.

Findings. The quality of teaching at the University of Wisconsin–Madison is generally high, as judged by student evaluations and peer observations. Nonetheless, professional pressures, the reward system for faculty members, and inadequate support have created a climate for teaching that is cause for serious concern. Other universities with a strong research mission have begun to address the climate for teaching by addressing the imbalance in the amount of professional recognition given to the four major components of academic work: (1) the discovery of new knowledge (research); (2) the integration of new knowledge with existing knowledge, both within a discipline and among disciplines; (3) the transmission of knowledge to students through teaching in classrooms, in laboratories, and in the field; and (4) the application of knowledge to practical problems.

The committee finds that the climate for teaching at the University of Wisconsin–Madison could be improved by alterations in current practice. The committee recommends eleven measures, which, we believe, will achieve higher quality in teaching and strike a better balance of effort in the four activities of scholarship, which are integral to our university mission.

The recommended changes in the system of teaching evaluation are designed primarily to improve the quality. At the same time, we believe, the recommended measures will address, in an appropriate way, the growing concerns of the public for accountability. Better measures of teaching performance and effective measures of learning will provide the basis for efforts to improve effectiveness at the same time that they offer the public better evidence of the seriousness of our commitment to excellence in teaching and learning. We believe that a system that is designed to reward excellence in teaching will focus some of the creativity, which is present on this campus, toward generating excellence in teaching and a climate for the sharing of ideas, which are two of the benefits from attending a great university.

Recommendations. The committee's recommendations are as follows:

1. Colleges, schools, departments, and programs, as appropriate to their respective missions, should allocate at least 20 percent of the annual merit pool to reward excellence in teaching. In addition, each college should allocate a portion of the dean's special merit pool to faculty members who have received university teaching awards in the past three years and who have maintained a record of teaching excellence. [Approved]

2. The University of Wisconsin–Madison and the University of Wisconsin System should continue their support of teaching improvement grants, university teaching awards, and sabbaticals dedicated to the renewing or developing of knowledge that will be used in teaching. [Approved]

3. The University of Wisconsin–Madison should create a teaching academy, composed of former recipients of the university teaching awards. Each recipient should serve a minimum of three years as a member of the teaching academy. The Office of the Provost should provide funding to the teaching academy so that it can hold seminars and workshops and produce or gather materials that support good teaching and learning. [Approved]

4. Colleges, schools, departments, and programs should initiate and support opportunities for faculty members to discuss teaching and the results of innovative approaches to learning. [Approved]

5. Expectations for student learning within disciplines and across disciplines should be reviewed on a regular basis, to keep pace with the changing shape of knowledge. Therefore, each department or program should periodically reexamine and redefine the purposes of its courses and

the relationships of those courses to one another and to courses offered outside the department or program. The results of these reviews should be conveyed to relevant departments, programs, and deans so that students may have a better understanding of the relationship of various courses to their possible choices of career or learning objectives. [Approved]

6. Departments and programs should design work assignments for faculty that encourage the scholarship of integration and interdisciplinary scholarship. [Approved]

7. Departments and other units where faculty members hold appointments should create a mechanism through which a faculty member could propose a personal short-term (for example, three-year) work plan that states the goals and a plan for a division of efforts among specific teaching, research, and service projects that serve the mission of the department and the university. [Approval pending]

8. Departments, schools, colleges, the university, the University of Wisconsin System, the regents, and the legislature should examine and seek to remove impediments to effective teaching, such as lack of instructional expendable supplies, inadequate access to duplicating, inadequate access to instructional technology, poorly maintained classrooms, unavailability of classrooms appropriate to class activity, and lack of personnel to enhance the processes of teaching and learning. [Approved]

9. Departments and programs should evaluate faculty performance in teaching and learning every year for probationary faculty and at least once every three years for tenured faculty on the basis of (a) performance of assigned duties in relation to the unit mission and (b) effectiveness of learning as indicated by as many of the following as appropriate: student perceptions of their learning process, measurement of student preparation for subsequent classes, student performance in relation to departmental expectations, peer evaluation of classroom teaching, peer evaluation of the contents of a self-prepared "teaching dossier," or similar document. [Approval pending]

10. Departments, schools, colleges, and appropriate administrative offices should work together to improve instruments for evaluating the effectiveness of teaching and learning and initiate corrective action if those evaluations indicate problems. Each instructor should use a student questionnaire, as suggested by the appropriate divisional committee, in every course taught every semester. [First part approved, second part approval pending]

11. After three years, the University Committee should recreate a committee of this type to focus on the issues of teaching quality, evaluation, and rewards in order to assess progress in implementing the recommendations and to suggest new recommendations for the next three-year period. [Approval pending]

Contact: David Ward, interim chancellor; telephone: (608) 262-9947.

Examining the Pressures:
Virginia Commonwealth University

Virginia Commonwealth University describes itself in its 1989 mission statement as a public, urban research university dedicated to learning, teaching, research, creative expression, and public service. In the spring of 1992, the provost convened a committee, chaired by Steven Robbibs and John Povlishock, to examine the relationship and balance between the institution's mission and its system of rewarding faculty. As this committee's report says, "An institution's system of faculty roles and rewards must balance individual aspirations and abilities against the institutional mission." Campus interest was stimulated in part by a survey of faculty that included the following issue: "In the immediate future, only modest resource increases will be available for use in the traditionally defined reward system."

This committee began with an examination of the pressures that affect the institution's shape and direction. The statement about these pressures presented here is an especially well wrought example of an important first step in the process of change. Based on extensive faculty input and feedback, a revised draft will be presented to the president in late summer 1993.

Following is an excerpt from the *Report of the Committee on the Status of Faculty Roles and Rewards* (Committee on the Status of Faculty Roles and Rewards, 1992):

External and Internal Pressures Confronting Us. Before detailing our recommendations, action steps, and issues identified for further study, we felt that it was important to provide a larger context, including a description of the internal and external pressures that confront us.

External Pressures. The university is being buffeted by tremendous economic, educational, and social forces. Societal economic decline coupled with the reduced prestige of higher education (for example, anti-intellectual backlash and scandals in research and financial administration) has made universities vulnerable, as evidenced by our own painful budget reductions.

Economically, our institution has experienced a period of unprecedented state budgetary cuts totaling 20 percent. The commonwealth is under continuing pressure to meet escalating costs in prisons and corrections and in Medicare and Medicaid. The pending court case on federal retiree benefits and the potential litigation around discrepancies in K–12 education systems throughout the commonwealth further darken the future economic picture. It is unlikely that the budget reductions that we have experienced will be restored. It is also unlikely that we will witness significant yearly faculty salary increases funded by the commonwealth.

Research universities have been attacked for neglecting their undergraduate mission, during a time when student costs and enrollment projections are skyrocketing. The legislature is highly concerned about the projection of sixty-five thousand new college students by the turn of the century at a time when funds are not available. Tremendous pressure will be placed on research universities to effectively meet new undergraduate student growth without increased faculty lines and operating costs to support this growth.

Universities are being called on to assist in ameliorating the considerable social, health, and economic problems facing American society. As a cornerstone of American society, we have an obligation to respond to these challenges. Our mission as an urban research institution further underscores the relevance of our service activities.

Nationally, as well as at the State Council of Higher Education for Virginia, examination of faculty work load is becoming equal to the assessment of undergraduate outcomes as the priority evaluation and planning task for higher education. This increasing attention on faculty work load issues is not surprising given the tremendous economic and demographic pressures and the more easily quantifiable nature of work load estimates than of student outcomes assessment. The general assembly, by a few votes, narrowly avoided a bill to automatically increase teaching loads across the commonwealth. Our challenge is to explain what we do and to help the public understand how productive we are at our multiple functions and roles.

Internal Issues. As can be seen, the university is being called on to make difficult priority budget decisions, to encourage excellence within an expanding undergraduate education system, and to develop alternative revenue sources to help support faculty efforts and university initiatives. Our challenge is to achieve a balance between our multifaceted and interwoven missions: to support our graduate and undergraduate education programs, to achieve preeminence as a Level 1 doctoral research institution, and to provide public service within our urban setting.

Entrepreneurship rather than entitlement is becoming our corporate ethic as the impact of state budgetary reductions are fully absorbed. The danger of creating an overcompetitive or intellectually shallow environment must be guarded against. At the same time, without aligning faculty roles and rewards to priority needs the institution will lose its ability to respond to our changing environment.

The university is examining the relative priorities that faculty should give to teaching, research, and service, and how these priorities should vary across unit (for example, department, school, or college). This examination must incorporate an understanding that faculty live in two communities: The first relates to our role as members of a scholarly community with allegiance to disciplines and scholarly fields. The second relates to membership in the university community, as professors with campus-defined obligations for teaching, research, and service. We believe that it is possible to better integrate our obligations and roles within both communities.

Reports on the faculty work load and status of interdisciplinary centers and the strategic planning process represented by the Commission on the Future of the University and the Health Sciences Campus Strategic Planning Group point to our efforts at examining faculty obligations or work roles. These efforts ultimately serve as a means of articulating, both internally and externally, who we are, what we do, how we do it, and where we should go.

Organization of the Report. We offer four basic recommendations beginning with the premise that the department is the key change unit, and that faculty within each unit must create individualized performance plans that are personally meaningful, central to department life, and consistent with our institutional mission. Faculty must be fairly and accurately evaluated and excellent performance must have incentives and rewards clearly tied to it.

RECOMMENDATION 1: *The department must become the unit of planning and evaluation.*

Rationale. Across the country, faculty see themselves facing a dilemma, torn between loyalty to their disciplines and loyalty to their institutions. At Virginia Commonwealth University, we face this national problem within the context of our own, unique moment. Our strategic planning will soon result in both a focused vision for the university and specific strategies for making it a reality. As part of this process, departments are the reasonable intermediary between institutional mission and the faculty member. Departments have been asked to evaluate themselves, and it is appropriate that we view each department as a team with a collective purpose and collective responsibility to meet university needs and achieve its mission. The responsibility will not be the same in every department; teaching loads, for example, will vary by departments, as will overall work loads that include research and public service. The differing roles and functions of departments and schools must be clearly articulated, so that each can be judged by standards appropriate to it and resources can be allocated appropriately.

RECOMMENDATION 2: *Begin a system of individualized performance planning keyed to departmental mission as the basis for faculty roles, evaluation, and reward.*

Rationale. A system of individualized performance planning would motivate faculty to develop in conjunction with their strengths and talents by incorporating professional changes and/or developments in more flexible career plans. The faculty member's choices or emphases would be mediated by the overall need for a balance of teaching, research, and service at the departmental, school, and university levels. An improved system might promote a more comprehensive and productive use of the faculty member's resources, benefiting the students, the university, and the individual faculty member. Such a system might enhance departmental or unit flexibility by planning to use faculty resources for common goals, increasing the productivity and quality.

RECOMMENDATION 3: *Chairs and their faculty must develop written performance criteria that articulate standards of excellence in teaching, research, and service.*

Rationale. To address the balance between faculty roles and rewards, it is clear that more must be done to better define the nature of faculty work, while designing innovative ways to document faculty performance. Superficially, this would seem a straightforward task; yet, on close examination, the task appears both complex and laden with pitfalls and shortcomings. Part of the problem stems from the current national debate regarding the nature of faculty work and the value assigned to it. Some are arguing that we reconceptualize the work of the professorship in terms of broader notions of scholarship in order to increase the status and reward related to teaching and service. Even if one were to agree on the precise nature of faculty work, further difficulty arises in identifying the criteria by which excellence in these endeavors would be determined. As the criteria for faculty excellence vary widely across disciplines, it must be questioned whether a standard set of performance criteria can be adopted across the university. Perhaps certain common markers of excellence can be identified; yet, additional concerns arise as to what specific criteria for establishing excellence would be used. Will the system merely continue to focus on quantitative measures of assessment, confining analysis to the number of lectures given, the number of papers published and the total hours of service provided, or will the system begin to consider qualitative aspects focusing on the impact of the scholarly, teaching, and service-related activities?

RECOMMENDATION 4: *The institution must develop a system of both salary and nonsalary rewards consistent with and supportive of the recommendations of faculty roles and evaluation.*

Rationale. The standardized use of performance plans as well as methods and criteria for evaluation will require the implementation of an appropriate and equitable reward system. All are cognizant that the attraction of academia lies in many scholarly and personal rewards that transcend simple monetary compensation; yet, it is also apparent that faculty who perform in accordance with the university's mission must be justly compensated for their efforts. Further, if excellence in teaching, research, and service is to be encouraged, an equitable and adequate reward structure must exist. Unfortunately, current economic projections do not suggest that significant salary raises are in the offing. If this is indeed the case, the question is how we can do a better job with the resources available to encourage and reward faculty performance and accomplishment. Perhaps, the answer lies in the use of both salary and nonsalary incentives, allowing faculty to be partially rewarded with salary incentives while receiving additional nonsalary perquisites that would benefit the individual's teaching and/or scholarly growth.

Contact: David Hiley, dean; telephone: (804) 367-1674.

Defining Scholarship at a Liberal Arts College: St. Norbert College

St. Norbert College, in DePere, Wisconsin, is a well-respected liberal arts school that holds the teaching-learning process as its primary focus. The three academic divisions of natural sciences, social sciences, and humanities and fine arts offer degrees in 47 majors, with 149 faculty and 1,877 students.

In 1991, the dean of the college, Robert Horn, appointed the Task Force on Defining Scholarship. This faculty committee researched the evolution of scholarship in the United States, read *Scholarship Reconsidered: Priorities for the Professoriate* (Boyer, 1990), conducted interviews, and surveyed the entire faculty as background to the development of a definition for the campus. With input from an open forum of faculty, the task force drafted and revised the definition. The faculty approved the definition in February 1992.

The newly adopted definition of scholarship was advanced to the personnel committee to modify promotion and tenure guidelines to reflect the broadened definition. The modified guidelines were approved by the faculty in December 1992. The definition of scholarship at St. Norbert College (with its accompanying rationale) is presented below as an example of both the process and the product of the struggle to define the work of faculty at liberal arts colleges.

Following is *A Definition of Scholarship at St. Norbert College* (Task Force on Defining Scholarship, 1992) in its entirety:

Concept of Scholarship. Scholarship at St. Norbert College is not an abstract term, but rather a way of life. It is a shared philosophy that deeply values the idea of a community of teacher-scholars learning and growing together—a community where cooperation rather than competition is the norm; a community where faculty-student learning partnerships are the goal; a community enfleshing the "mutual respect and trust" to which our mission statement refers.

The concept of scholarship at St. Norbert College recognizes the value of all who strive to bring light into the corners of darkness, of all who join the struggle to push back the boundaries of ignorance that surround us. This includes not only the explorers who expand the frontiers of knowledge, but also the pioneers who help define the boundaries, construct the maps, and build the roads connecting the various provinces in the new realm. And while our definition reflects our individuality as a small liberal arts college whose reason for being is to help undergraduate students learn, it also recognizes the traditional concept of scholarship informing the wider realm of academia.

In essence, scholarship at St. Norbert College is the bringing to bear of a trained mind on a problem or question and the public sharing of the results of those labors. It is what academics *do*. It demands training, clear and objective thinking, synthesis, creativity, and an ability and willingness to communicate. It implies originality, discovery, testing, convincing, and debating. It explores new territory, builds on what is known, or interprets what is given. It may be seminal, or add a simple footnote. It can be done alone or in teams, but it is *done;* there is a result, an offering.

At the very heart of the St. Norbert definition of scholarship is the concept of intellectual vitality and growth. A scholar is an active learner, not a person who passively rests on past accomplishments. In effect, scholars manifest the best qualities of exemplary students: They ask questions, seek answers, look for connections, engage in problem solving, and apply what they have learned. Good scholars, like good students, demonstrate a lifelong commitment to continuing self-education.

Process of Scholarship. Also central to the definition of scholarship at St. Norbert College is the belief that scholarship is not only a product, a result, a "contribution to the field," but also the sometimes lengthy process that precedes, generates, and shapes the "product." It is this process that sustains and, to some extent, defines the intellectual vitality of both the teacher-scholar and the liberal arts college. Scholarship, therefore, includes researching, learning, exploring, reflecting, and experimenting. However, a fruitful process is not intermittent, random, or fragmented, but instead sustained, focused, and integrated.

The process of scholarship, while it may be an individual pursuit, need not be undertaken in isolation. The scholar should consciously seek a dialogue with colleagues, both inside and outside the college, who can serve as guides, commentators, and evaluators. That is, scholarly work (whether completed or in process) should be periodically and publicly shared and submitted to the scrutiny of one's peers. This sharing is essential in maintaining the integrity of the scholarly process. In short, scholarship involves the acquisition and advancement of knowledge and the exposure of such efforts to the critical evaluation of others.

Stages of Scholarship. Although scholarship is a complex organic process, three closely interrelated and sometimes overlapping stages are discernible:

Self-Development. In this stage of scholarship, learning takes place on a regular basis through such means as reading articles and books, attending professional meetings, and discussing field-related topics with colleagues. Such self-development helps the scholar to grow personally, intellectually, and professionally. This stage may be more pronounced in the early career of a scholar, but does not end there. Self-development through learning continues unabated throughout a scholar's life.

Productivity. During this stage, the scholar's learning is brought to fruition. As a result of intellectual and professional growth, a scholar may, for example, write manuscripts, prepare a grant proposal, develop software, create a work of art, interpret existing artistic works, or devise effective strategies for making knowledge comprehensible to others. The nature of scholarly engagement in this stage may change throughout a scholar's professional life, but the self-development stage should naturally result in some form of regular productivity in one's career.

Dissemination. In this stage, the scholar shares the products of scholarship with the academic community through such media as performance, publication, exhibition, workshops, and public or professional presentations. This sharing enables the scholar to improve the work, contribute to existing scholarship, and continue to grow as scholar, teacher, and professional.

Aims of Scholarship. Listed below are four general aims of scholarship. Underlying each aim is the assumption that scholars make evident the process of scholarship through communication and sharing with colleagues, peers, or the public. These four scholarly aims are distinct from teaching, even though in some ways they may be closely related. The examples for each type of scholarship are illustrative in nature and not definitive.

The creation or discovery of new knowledge, insights, or works: This type of activity not only enhances the intellectual climate of the college but augments its prestige as a center for higher learning. As Ernest Boyer (1990) points out in *Scholarship Reconsidered,* "No tenets in the academy are held in higher regard than the commitment to knowledge for its own sake, to freedom of inquiry, and to following, in a disciplined fashion, an investigation wherever it may lead." Examples of this type of scholarship include research projects, musical or theatrical performances, and artistic or literary creations.

The creation or discovery of innovative pedagogical techniques: This type of activity may include more traditional educational research, which "seeks to discover and validate general laws of teaching and learning," or classroom research, which seeks "to provide faculty with information and insights into what, how, and how well their particular students are learning in their specific courses" (Angelo, 1991, p. 8). Although focusing on pedagogy, this kind of practice-based inquiry may also encompass curriculum innovations that help generate new teaching-learning techniques. Examples of this type of scholarship might include (1) developing new instructional models for classes composed of culturally diverse students, (2) conducting a comparative study of teaching-learning strategies in a team-taught interdisciplinary course in an attempt to enhance the effectiveness of the students' learning experience, and (3) analyzing the effects of using humor in the classroom.

The development of a novel integration of preexisting information or ideas: The integrative process builds bridges between two previously unconnected topics, helps interpret data and information, gives meaning to new discoveries and original research, and may even lead to the discovery of new knowledge. The scholarship of integration may include, but is not limited to, cross-disciplinary research, the development of interdisciplinary courses, and artistic creations and performances featuring a cross-disciplinary orientation. Specific examples of integrative scholarship may include such academic exercises as using computer technology to analyze poetry, bringing ethical principles to bear on biotechnology, and applying psychoanalytic theory to the study of literature or marketing.

The application of theoretical knowledge to consequential problems that results in new knowledge or innovative solutions to the problems: In this form of scholarship the scholar applies specialized knowledge to a significant problem to yield new knowledge and to concurrently solve or reduce the problem. Examples of this kind of scholarship are (1) applying economic theory to existing tax law to propose revisions intended to facilitate more efficient allocation of resources and promote economic growth, (2) applying new theory developed in successful alternative schools to reduce dropout in traditional comprehensive schools, and (3) applying the principles of food web ecology of lakes to the problems associated with surplus nutrients and algal growth in an attempt to improve water quality. As Ernest Boyer (1990) suggests, "In activities such as these, theory and practice vitally interact, and one renews the other."

While effective teaching-learning is the primary focus at St. Norbert College, we must also recognize the vital importance of sustaining the intellectual growth and development of all faculty. This dynamism may take different forms, but it must exist. Without it we fail ourselves, our students, our institution, and the wider realm of academe. Active scholarship is consistent with the mission and the spirit of community of St. Norbert College.

Contact: Robert L. Horn, vice president for academic affairs and dean of the college; telephone: (414) 337-3001.

An Integrated Approach: Syracuse University

Aware that the quality of the undergraduate experience would not improve until the faculty reward system recognized the importance of quality teaching, Syracuse University sought a small grant from the Sears-Roebuck

Foundation in 1989 to begin establishing an appropriate balance between teaching and research. Support for the project has continued with the commitment of the central administration and the involvement of deans, chairs, and faculty. In addition, the project has expanded to address the issues of service, advising, and broadening of the definition of scholarly and professional work.

The goal of the one-year Sears Project (as it became known on campus) was to enhance the perceived importance of undergraduate teaching at the university. The project had three purposes related to this goal: First, to help deans and department chairs gain a better understanding of how they influence the attitudes and priorities of faculty regarding teaching; second, to assist them in identifying the various activities and resources available to influence attitudes and priorities; and third, to indicate ways in which the central administration could support deans and chairs in these efforts.

The decision to focus the effort on deans and chairs was pragmatic, based on two major factors. First, these administrators are essential in initiating changes in both programs and faculty attitudes. As faculty leaders, deans and chairs have direct influence on instructional effectiveness since their guidance and encouragement largely determines the level of effort that faculty devote to their teaching. In addition, deans and chairs create faculty members' perceptions of priorities and rewards, establish departmental norms regarding the importance of teaching, and allocate instructional resources. Second, the size of Syracuse University (fourteen schools and colleges with over seventy-five departments and academic divisions) demanded that change be implemented efficiently and effectively. Deans and chairs brought this effort to faculty campuswide in their working units.

Activities. The following is a brief chronicle of activities pursued in Syracuse's integrated approach to change.

Advisory Board Established, Fall 1988. Project codirectors Ronald Cavanagh and Robert M. Diamond established a board consisting of administrators, deans, chairs, professional staff from the Center for Instructional Development, and faculty members who had served in administrative roles.

Survey of Perceptions as to the Relative Importance of Undergraduate Teaching and Research, March 1989. As a first step, faculty, deans, and chairs were asked their perceptions of the balance between teaching and research at Syracuse University, the direction they felt the institution was moving, and the balance that they would consider to be ideal. The survey had four main purposes: to provide data on the present climate of the institution, to identify strengths and weaknesses of the present reward system, to provide baseline data so that changes over time could be tracked, and, perhaps most important, to place the question of the balance between teaching and research on the institutional agenda. The survey revealed a perceived overemphasis on research at the expense of teaching and raised a number of other issues that needed to be addressed.

A summary report on the data from this survey (Gray, Froh, and Diamond, 1992), which was subsequently administered at 47 research universities, is available by writing the Center for Instructional Development at Syracuse. The survey, under a grant from the Lilly Endowment, is now being administered at over 180 institutions representing all Carnegie classifications. A report is expected in spring 1994.

Seminar for Deans and Chairs on Undergraduate Teaching. A two-day meeting was held at an off-campus center. Topics covered at the conference included the status of higher education in the United States, an overview of national problems, a report of the campus survey results, a discussion of the roles of chairs and deans in the support of teaching, and a review of the role of evaluation in improving instruction. Time was set aside at the conference for deans and their respective chairs to develop school and college action plans to improve teaching in their units. Participants were also asked to make recommendations to the central administration regarding actions that it could take to support teaching.

Improving Teaching: A Book of Readings for Deans and Department Chairs. A book of readings discussing the roles of deans and chairs in improving teaching was distributed at the seminar.

Meetings with Deans and Chairs, Fall 1989. The deans and chairs from each school or college began discussions with faculty on the action plans developed at the summer conference. Modification of the existing promotion and tenure guidelines began in some units. Several groups developed teaching support programs for new faculty during this period. A major area of concern that surfaced during these meetings was the existing emphasis on a narrow definition of research. Most professional programs reported that the "traditional approach" to research and scholarship was often inappropriate in their fields. As a result, they reported that some work was not given adequate weight in the reward system.

Focus on Teaching Conference, December 1989. Over one hundred deans, associate deans, academic directors, and chairs attended this half-day conference, which began with a presentation by Russell Edgerton, president of the American Association of Higher Education. He focused on professional service activities and recommended their inclusion in the faculty evaluation process. Several schools and colleges reported that they had formulated (and in some cases implemented) specific programs from their action plans. Also, a faculty instructional grants program was announced, and administrative commitments were made to improve the instructional quality of specific courses.

Conference on Evaluating Teaching for Deans, Chairs, and Nominated Faculty Serving on Promotion and Tenure Committees, August 1990. At the invitation of the chancellor, over 135 administrators and faculty members participated in a one-day workshop just before the start of classes. Four department chairs distributed detailed information about the teaching evaluation plans that their departments had developed. Following these discussions, the deans met with their chairs and faculty participants to begin developing plans for programs to evaluate teaching effectiveness. The final session of the summer workshop introduced the professional portfolio, which was recommended for possible use by school-year faculty in prepara- tion for their third-year review and for use by promotion and tenure committees.

Individual Schools, Colleges, and Departments Develop Standards and Procedures for Evaluating Teaching, 1990 to Present. During this period a number of activities took place: on-campus and off-campus publications focused on the project; a major portion of the chancellor's annual report (his last before retirement) was devoted to the importance of teaching and to this project; Ernest Boyer, president of the Carnegie Foundation for the Advance- ment of Teaching, spoke to the faculty on "the new American scholar" (spring 1991); a workshop on the redefinition of research and scholarship was held, with Eugene Rice as principal speaker. As academic units began developing their promotion and tenure guidelines, they were encouraged to develop protocols that would be specific to the discipline; recognize the strengths of the individuals; respond to the priorities of the school, college, or department; recognize that, over time, priorities change; and recognize that the desired balance between teaching and research may be achieved at the school, college, or departmental level. It was anticipated that each school and college would proceed in a manner that was appropriate for its size and governing structure.

A New Chancellor, an Increased Emphasis (Fall 1992). The effort to pay greater attention to the undergraduate experience and to develop a more balanced approach to the promotion and tenure system was to become a major focus of Chancellor Kenneth A. Shaw's program initiatives. His first major address included a number of specific initiatives designed to continue and expand on the effort to improve the quality of teaching and to review the tenure and promotion system. His formal report, presented to the university in February 1992, contained a number of specific references to these initiatives as well as target dates for the schools and colleges to submit revised promotion, tenure, and merit salary guidelines. The focus on teaching and a redefinition of scholarly work was bolstered further with a January 1993 memorandum to the academic deans from Vice Chancellor Gershon Vincow, who requested "that each tenure case considered in the future explicitly evaluate the contributions of the faculty member to lower-division under- graduate advising, undergraduate majors advising, and graduate advising (including thesis and dissertation supervision) and include a statement concerning this evaluation in the file which is forwarded to me." The memorandum concluded, "As we continue to seek ways of improving advising and mentoring of students, it is essential that we give this aspect of 'teaching and learning' appropriate recognition in the faculty reward system.

I encourage the school and college committees to give similar treatment to advising and mentoring in their deliberation concerning faculty promotion."

Impact. As noted, deans and chairs were to play a major role in the development and implementation of departmental mission statements and revised tenure and promotion guidelines. While each dean selected a process that was most appropriate for his or her unit, their leadership roles were essential to the success of this effort. By the early spring of 1993, a number of schools, colleges, and departments had met with their faculty to revise their unit mission statements and implement new promotion and tenure guidelines and procedures for the evaluation of teaching.

Contact: Robert M. Diamond, assistant vice chancellor for instructional development; telephone: (315) 443-4571.

Campuses Working Together to Initiate Change: The Focus on Teaching Project

In early 1990, following from the work under way at Syracuse University, Alton O. Roberts of the Center for Instructional Development proposed a collaborative approach to change at six research universities. The project was supported by the Fund for the Improvement of Postsecondary Education (FIPSE) and included participation by the University of California at Berkeley, Carnegie-Mellon University, the University of Massachusetts at Amherst, Northwestern University, Ohio State University, and the University of Michigan.

The ultimate goal of the Focus on Teaching Project was to improve the learning experiences of thousands of students at these institutions, using an institutional change and leadership development approach with several specific objectives and activities: (1) use the national study (Gray, Froh, and Diamond, 1992) to examine perceptions of faculty and administrators on each campus regarding the relative importance of teaching and research, (2) provide a forum for academic leaders on each campus to address the improvement of instruction, (3) facilitate the creation of action plans that place greater weight on undergraduate teaching and are specific to key academic units in the participating institutions, (4) identify and develop support systems to provide instructional assistance on each campus and collectively, (5) identify existing reward systems and encourage development of new ones so that greater weight is placed on undergraduate teaching and advising, and (6) assist academic units in developing a definition of creativity and scholarship for use in tenure and promotion decisions that reflects the nature of the discipline and the creative and scholarly aspects of teaching-related activities.

The Focus on Teaching Project was designed to build on the experiences at Syracuse but not to replicate them. After reviewing the process of change introduced at Syracuse, the campus teams developed action plans for their particular institutions. Common among all campus plans were the use of the national study, the establishment of a campus advisory committee, and the identification of a campus coordinator.

Through the Focus on Teaching Project, the campus coordinators met to discuss ways to enlist the support of key campus academic leaders to serve on the campus advisory committee. The next major activity was to bring all of the campus advisory committee members together (about sixty people) to a meeting in San Antonio to confer on the change process and discuss plans for the campus programs—the central activity of the project. Most campuses then planned a local one- or two-day retreat for deans and chairs where action plans would be designed to enhance the importance of teaching.

Two subprojects developed from the project meetings and were subsequently funded by FIPSE as parts of the grant. The first was the attempt to develop discipline-specific definitions of scholarship (see Adam and Roberts, this volume). The other was the beginning of a study to better understand what influences faculty professional behavior, especially intrinsic motivation (see Froh, Menges, and Walker, this volume).

As the Focus on Teaching Project progressed, a number of procedural differences among the institutions appeared. While several campuses published detailed reports on the data from the national study for distribution to the entire campus, others reported this information more locally through deans and academic chairs. There were also differences in the ways in which the advisory committees were constituted and the ways in which they chose to work within their campus communities. On several campuses, administrative changes affected the initiatives that were introduced and the time line of the project. Finally, implementation strategies were influenced by the administrative structure and style and the governing practices of the institutions.

After two and a half years of meetings and activities, each of the six campuses has had much to report. An overview of the activities at each of the institutions is presented below, along with the name of the campus coordinator.

University of Massachusetts, Amherst. The chancellor's and deans' offices have initiated an expanded set of teaching awards. The purpose of the College Outstanding Teaching Award is to honor faculty members in each college for teaching accomplishments. The Faculty Senate Committee on Teaching Evaluation and Improvement is focusing its attention on two projects: the design of a teaching portfolio plan and a flexible student evaluation of teaching form. The Center for Teaching received funding from the Lilly Endowment to bring together excellent teachers in the northeastern United States to share ideas about teaching in a collegial forum.

The provost appointed members to the Faculty Working Group on Academic Advising and Support Services; the group currently is addressing issues raised in a report of the Undergraduate Retention Committee. The provost's office sponsored a second conference on undergraduate education and multiculturalism. The provost also appointed two new ad hoc committees. One is looking at the annual faculty review plan and will recommend changes to specifically recognize broader-based teaching and multicultural contributions. The other will look at ways to create, recognize, and reward interdisciplinary efforts in both teaching and research.

Coordinator: Mary Deane Sorcinelli, Center for Teaching.

Carnegie-Mellon University. Carnegie-Mellon appointed a new president and provost and created a new position, vice provost for undergraduate education. The vice provost is the primary academic officer responsible for reviving leadership and innovation in undergraduate education, one of the major commitments of the new administration.

The Commission for Undergraduate Education was established with a charge to improve student learning and faculty teaching and to create an atmosphere of scholarship and excitement that transcends the classroom. Task forces of this commission are discussing such issues as the enhancement of support services for faculty and students and the faculty reward system. The Commission on Undergraduate Education is currently making recommendations to the university, colleges, and departments on these issues.

Coordinator: Susan Ambrose, University Teaching Center.

Ohio State University. The Academy on Teaching, composed of recipients of the Alumni Distinguished Teaching Award, was established. Responsibilities of academy members include mentoring young faculty, preparing graduate students for teaching, and serving as "teaching ambassadors" for the university, which entails generating resources to support teaching and serving as advisers to the Office of Academic Affairs and the colleges and departments in matters of teaching evaluation.

The provost's Committee on Teaching will advise the provost on ways to improve the teaching environment. Other groups to advise the provost include a committee on faculty dossiers and another on promotion and tenure procedures. As part of the Intrinsic Motivation Study, a subproject of the Focus on Teaching Project, a seminar, Maintaining Faculty Viability in Teaching, was presented. The Center for Teaching Excellence developed a compendium of examples of teaching support, including faculty development, evaluation, and reward strategies. This resource was compiled from department and college reports.

Coordinator: Anne Pruitt, Center for Teaching Excellence.

University of California, Berkeley. In the area of evaluating and rewarding teaching, a culture of teaching excellence is being created on campus. A statewide task force published the *Pister Report,* emphasizing documentation of teaching effectiveness, including peer evaluation, and endorsing the recognition of faculty for mentoring and advising activities.

The Academic Senate Committee on Budget and Interdepartmental Relations implemented a policy that rewards senior faculty for teaching excellence.

In the area of awards and recognition, the Educational Initiatives Award was established. This award will be given to a group of faculty (a department, program, and so on) in recognition of significant accomplishment in undergraduate education. A three-year endowed chair has been established for one or two faculty members to develop educational initiatives for freshmen and sophomores.

In the area of undergraduate teaching initiatives, Berkeley has expanded freshman seminars and undergraduate research programs, established academic centers in all residence halls, and introduced an electronic mail forum for exchanging information, advice, and questions about teaching.

Coordinator: Barbara Gross Davis, Office of Educational Development.

Northwestern University. The Teaching Excellence Center was established to serve the university's undergraduate schools, a major hard money commitment to teaching. A $10 million endowment established ten professorships to honor outstanding teachers.

Several of the undergraduate schools are revising procedures for documenting teaching for salary, promotion, and tenure review. Curriculum experiments, including junior tutorials and courses that carry fractional credits, were introduced following recommendations of a task force on undergraduate education.

Coordinator: Robert J. Menges, Center for the Teaching Professions.

University of Michigan. The new faculty orientation includes workshops specifically addressing faculty rewards for teaching and research. Focus groups on teaching and research have also been established. The Undergraduate Research Opportunity Program was established to bring undergraduates in direct contact with research faculty in order to enhance the teaching of those faculty in a mutually productive manner. A year-long program was developed for engineering faculty that emphasizes the importance of teaching. A program for new faculty in the College of Literature, Science, and the Arts provides the opportunity for midsemester teaching evaluation, with feedback, designed to improve performance and communicate the importance of teaching.

Winners of teaching awards from the past five years were brought together for a discussion of the intrinsic rewards experienced in their teaching and to advise the Center for Research on Learning and Teaching on how the university might convey more strongly to faculty the value of teaching. A university retreat was held in May 1993 that focused on the faculty reward structure. The keynote speaker was David Scott, former provost and currently professor of physics at Michigan State University.

Coordinator: Donald Brown, Center for Research on Learning and Teaching.

Other Campuses Active in Change

The following sample of institutions represents the range of activities that are now part of the fabric of so many institutions of higher education. Along with a very brief account of each institution's activity, we include the name of a person to contact for further information.

California State University, Long Beach. In 1991, the provost created the Advisory Commission on the Functions and Values of Teaching, Scholarly, and Creative Activity and University and Community Service. It was charged with taking a broad look at the relevance of scholarship and community service to teaching, the contributions that each of the three make to the university's mission, and ways in which faculty performance standards might be articulated. A report released in June 1992 contains recommendations in four areas: a broadened definition of scholarship, using Boyer's four categories; faculty empowerment, by recognizing growth and change over a faculty member's career and various faculty specializations among the scholarship categories; realistic expectations, given available levels of support; and faculty career plans, beginning at the point of hire and renewed every four years.

Contact: Marilyn Jensen, associate vice president for academic affairs; telephone: (310) 985-4128.

University of Cincinnati. In 1991, in response to both internal and external pressures, a team of administrators and faculty leaders decided to establish a task force on faculty work load. The group was created to address how to (1) achieve equity and fairness across the university, (2) explain to external audiences what the faculty do as professionals, and (3) determine if any budget savings can be achieved. Approximately twenty-five faculty members representing all academic units developed a report that was issued in the spring of 1992. The report addressed all three of the above charges, including a mandate that "all academic programs formalize and clarify their criteria and procedures to assure that all faculty members within the program have comparable workloads as workload has been defined in this document." The council of deans later endorsed the report, and the Faculty Senate endorsed the development of unit-level policies consistent with the report.

Contact: Maria Kreppel, vice provost for faculty; telephone: (513) 556-4692.

University of Georgia. During the past several years, the university has been engaged in a number of projects pertinent to faculty roles and rewards. First, guidelines for promotion and tenure were revised in 1992; notable within these is the acknowledgment that faculty may have responsibilities that focus heavily on one of the three traditional functions of teaching, service, and research, and that the quality of their performance must be judged accordingly. Evidence for promotion on the basis of teaching excellence must, however, also involve "creative and transportable developments in instruction," not just classroom performance. Second, a special professorship, the University Professor, was created to reward faculty members with distinguished contributions to the university in areas other than creative scholarship. Third, opportunities have been created for encouraging faculty members' instructional efforts, including instructional technology grants, teaching fellows programs, and instructional awards for junior faculty.

Contact: William F. Prokasy, vice president for academic affairs; telephone: (706) 542-5806.

Indiana University–Purdue University at Indianapolis. In 1988, a faculty task force was charged with conducting a comprehensive review of faculty appointments and advancements. The committee issued a report in 1992 based on extensive surveys, consultations, and discussions. The report contains over thirty recommendations, covering such topics as criteria and standards for tenure; procedures for faculty recruitment, orientation, and performance reviews; production and character of dossiers (including a recommendation that resources be made available to advise faculty on their preparation); procedures for posttenure review; development options and incentives for senior faculty; and retirement issues. After campuswide review, a number of the recommendations were implemented: improved faculty orientation program highlighting the criteria for promotion and tenure, development of more detailed procedures for faculty rewards at the departmental level, implementation of a formal, institutionwide three-year faculty review and feedback program, and requirement that all units implement a three-year term of service on promotion and tenure committees. Recommendations requiring formal faculty action will be submitted for approval in fall 1993.

Contact: William M. Plater, dean of the faculties; telephone: (317) 274-4500.

Kent State University. Since 1988, three major projects have been undertaken related to faculty rewards. First, the Review Committee for Merit Pay, an ad hoc committee of the Faculty Senate, conducted surveys of other institutions and Kent State faculty members and released a report in 1989 that contained more than twenty major recommendations dealing with merit categories, respective roles of faculty committees and administrators, methods of evaluation, and appeal procedures. Second, with the appointment of Carol A. Cartwright as president in 1991, another senate ad hoc committee used *Scholarship Reconsidered: Priorities for the Professoriate* (Boyer, 1990) as a basis for the development of a position paper titled "Principles for Evaluation and Reward of Faculty Scholarship." Third, as part of a statewide effort to examine faculty productivity and work load, the university engaged in a comprehensive productivity study during the spring of 1992. Three unique aspects of the study were the use of Boyer's model as the framework for assessing faculty scholarship, use of departmental profiles rather than individual profiles to analyze faculty efforts, and use of faculty diaries to document in more qualitative ways the complexities of faculty work. The Kent State study was cited as a "best practice" by the Ohio Task Force on Managing for the Future.

Contact: Carol A. Cartwright, president; telephone: (216) 672-2210.

University of Louisville. The impetus for a new definition of faculty roles began with the university's first strategic plan in 1985, which required the university to develop "flexible arrangements for faculty positions." The revised plan in 1989, reflecting decreased state appropriations and increased external pressure for accountability, called for new programs to enhance productivity, and the president initiated a universitywide restructuring process. These steps resulted in two new objectives, each approved by the board: the development and implementation of a "less rigid definition of faculty" and the initiation of a process of posttenure review. After considerable discussion and negotiation between the provost and the Faculty Senate, a document was agreed on, stipulating that tenured faculty be permitted to "distribute their efforts in ways best suited to their strengths and the needs of their units, and to reconfigure that distribution as necessary over the course of their career," that "appropriate and equitable rewards" be secured for "all faculty effort that contributes to the University's mission," and that the process for posttenure review "serve for faculty development, not for punitive or budget-reduction purposes."

Contact: Wallace Mann, provost; telephone: (502) 588-6153; or Dale B. Billingsley; telephone: (502) 588-7598.

Murray State University. Emerging from a strategic planning process in 1990 were several initiatives focusing on the university's teaching and learning environment, including task forces to develop a comprehensive program to evaluate teaching, examine international education, examine the university's learning climate, and suggest how to improve the use of technology in learning. Other efforts stemming from the strategic plan include a statement of "intended exiting characteristics" for graduating students (a document that has been widely accepted by the university community and the board of regents) and a recommendation that faculty members be rewarded in ways that recognize their "unique and differentiated roles within their departments." In brief, the university has been undergoing a significant cultural change while facing several major problems. These include restrictive compensation policies, a declining budget, and campus resistance to some programs because they are viewed as top-down endeavors.

Contact: Gary Hunt, dean, College of Fine Arts and Communication; telephone: (502) 762-4516.

University of Nebraska. Faculty and administrators have been working on the problem of rewards for teaching for more than five years. Based on the efforts of a few faculty and administrators and work with a handful of departments, the project expanded with FIPSE support to encompass twenty-seven departments, each of which has developed written plans for rewarding teaching. Recently, ten more departments were added. Current literature on evaluation incorporating the portfolio approach and new ways of thinking about the scholarship of teaching have been prominent components of these plans. A two-year FIPSE grant (1992–1994) was awarded to the university to disseminate information on the process developed in the project to other universities. Relevant project documents include "From Regard to Reward: Improving Teaching at a Research University" and a Rewarding Teaching Project questionnaire.

Contact: Leverne Barrett, professor of agricultural leadership, education, and communications; telephone: (402) 472-2807; or Robert Narveson, professor of English; telephone: (402) 472-1808.

Pennsylvania State University. Several major initiatives have taken place in the past several years. In 1989, a task force on faculty development was charged to examine issues of "faculty activity, worth, and recognition, and to make recommendations in these areas." Recommendations of this group included criteria for promotion and tenure and an emphasis on faculty development from a "life-cycle perspective." Another task force reexamined the quality of undergraduate education, including among its recommendations that the university "reward excellent teaching unambiguously and at all locations with above-average merit pay and in the promotion and tenure process," and that sabbaticals for "pedagogical" purposes be encouraged. Outcomes of these task forces included a competitive salary program for "innovative collaborative teaching activities" and guidelines to assist faculty members preparing for pedagogical sabbaticals.

Contact: John A. Brighton, executive vice president and provost; telephone: (814) 865-2505.

Texas A&M University. In 1990, the Task Force on the Multiple Missions of the University was commissioned by President William Mobley to recommend how the various university missions should be appropriately "recognized, rewarded, and nurtured and how an appropriate balance could be maintained among these missions." The task force released its report in May 1991. Some of the key recommendations are the following: (1) Any changes in mission emphasis should be articulated annually by the president and reflected throughout academic planning at all levels. (2) A "community of scholars" should be the basis for the university's multiple missions. (3) The university should pursue its teaching and public service missions with resources equal to those given the research mission, even if this requires shifting of resources. (4) Graduate programs should include preparation for teaching. (5) All faculty members should be involved in undergraduate education. (6) The university should develop ways of encouraging and supporting interdisciplinary units devoted to scholarly or public policy issues. (7) Relatively greater attention should be given to contributions made by faculty members to the scholarly community, and relatively less to contributions to the disciplinary field. And (8) in the interest of continuous improvement, goals and measures should be established allowing assessment of institutional performance relative to mission.

Contact: William L. Perry, associate provost and dean of faculties; telephone: (409) 845-3210.

References

Angelo, T. A. "Introduction and Overview: From Classroom Assessment to Classroom Research." In T. A. Angelo (ed.), *Classroom Research: Early Lessons from Success.* New Directions for Teaching and Learning, no. 46. San Francisco: Jossey-Bass, 1991.

Barrows, R. *Elements for the Chancellor's Report to the System: 1992 Accomplishments, Suggested 1993 Goals.* Madison: University of Wisconsin, 1993.

Boyer, E. L. *Scholarship Reconsidered: Priorities for the Professoriate.* Princeton, N.J.: Carnegie Foundation for the Advancement of Teaching, 1990.

Committee on Teaching Quality, Evaluation, and Rewards. *Report of the Committee on Teaching Quality, Evaluation, and Rewards.* Madison: University of Wisconsin, 1992.

Committee on the Status of Faculty Roles and Rewards. *Report of the Committee on the Status of Faculty Roles and Rewards.* Richmond: Virginia Commonwealth University, 1992.

Gray, P. J., Froh, R. C., and Diamond, R. M. *A National Study of Research Universities on the Balance Between Research and Undergraduate Teaching.* Syracuse, N.Y.: Center for Instructional Development, Syracuse University, 1992.

Task Force on Defining Scholarship. *A Definition of Scholarship at St. Norbert College.* DePere, Wis.: St. Norbert College, 1992.

Alton O. Roberts is director of instructional design at the Center for Instructional Development, Syracuse University.

Jon F. Wergin is professor of education at Virginia Commonwealth University, Richmond.

Bronwyn E. Adam is assistant project director at the Center for Instructional Development, Syracuse University.

Conversations with faculty suggest ways in which a campus climate can be established to increase the intrinsic rewards of teaching.

Revitalizing Faculty Work Through Intrinsic Rewards

Robert C. Froh, Robert J. Menges, Charles J. Walker

The major focus of this volume is on the formal faculty reward system: promotion, tenure, and merit salary increases. There are, however, other factors that can play a major role in maximizing the effectiveness of faculty at colleges and universities. Many faculty chose careers in academia for reasons other than fiscal rewards. They enjoy working with younger people, they find the vigor of scholarly activity stimulating and the work with colleagues in their disciplines challenging, and they love teaching. Therefore, to change priorities in the nature and focus of academic activities, the characteristics of intrinsic rewards and the conditions under which they surface to influence faculty work must be understood. With this understanding, institutions and specific academic departments, as well as professional associations, can establish a climate that builds on these conditions to increase intrinsic rewards and improve the quality of faculty work.

A theory of intrinsic rewards is presented in this chapter to help faculty and institutions see how they can encourage and manage these rewards in a more systematic way. Research is presented that identified intrinsic rewards in teaching and the conditions under which these rewards can be increased. This research included telephone interviews with fifty-two faculty members at six prestigious research institutions and focus group interviews with thirty-six faculty at two of the original six institutions sampled.

Turning Faculty Work into Optimal Experiences

As Csikszentmihalyi (1990) has described, people who are most effective in obtaining intrinsic rewards for their efforts strive to (1) set goals where challenges are not too far ahead of their developing skills, and where feedback can be monitored to easily modify goals, (2) become immersed in the activity by finding a close mesh between the demands of the environment and their capacity to act, (3) pay attention to what is happening by maintaining concentration and deep involvement and by getting rid of self-consciousness, and (4) learn to enjoy immediate experience even when objective circumstances are difficult. When these conditions are operating, the experiences become optimal. Csikszentmihalyi calls them "flow experiences," when skills and challenges are nearly in balance—actually, when challenges can be adjusted so they are just ahead of skills. When skills are insufficient to the challenges of a task, anxiety builds. When the skills are more than is needed for completing the task, boredom ensues. When a person is capable of both higher skills and higher challenges than a task offers, apathy takes over. This theory suggests that faculty and institutions can increase the likelihood for optimal experiences in teaching and thereby maximize opportunities for intrinsic rewards.

Intrinsic Rewards in Teaching

The enjoyment associated with teaching can be related to a number of factors. In our focus groups, faculty described memorable moments in teaching when they and their students obtained new levels of understanding and mutual learning, they mastered the content and discipline at more satisfying levels, and they found new variations of teaching methods that helped students understand the material.

New Levels of Understanding and Mutual Learning. The highest percentage of the experiences that faculty described involve their work with students to obtain a new level of interaction and mutual learning (Menges, 1993). A professor teaching an ethics course talked about getting students to a high level of interaction and critical thinking:

> They were listening and paying attention and they were critically thinking of the issues that were going on. They were working hard and I think the whole group was energized and time tended not to matter at that particular time. No one looked bored. . . They were willing to share personal issues as well as professional experiences. . . . . There was a lot of exchange and I think they got to a higher level of critical thinking.

A professor in writing talked about a time when teaching core principles in the use of ethnography that "a student had assumed the authority to speak about this text," serving as a catalyst to get more interaction and understanding from other students:

> Over the course of the discussions one student had a particularly difficult time and read an ethnography from this textbook. He started critiquing

it and as he was going through this essay and he says no this not a good example of an ethnography and here are the reasons why. He just laid it out. Once he did that he looked at me and said, "right?" I said "right." The other students started to critique and look at the examples of ethnographers and to learn. I think they started figuring out that they could learn what was good ethnography and what was bad ethnography by doing this exercise.

A professor teaching a course in public speaking talked about the ways in which she got more investment in the course by getting students to share their reactions to the course at midsemester:

> One student would say, "I spend a couple of hours writing a speech and I don't think it is a problem," but another student would say, "I spent eight hours writing a speech and I think it is a problem." There was dialogue and they would stand up for what they believed in.

An English professor teaching a class in folklore talked about getting students to share personal examples in order to understand their own folklore, after lecturing "about how folklore of children has changed over the decades":

> I gave examples along with them doing their reading. They began to respond and give me examples of what was happening now. . . . Then we ended up with the kids talking about the kinds of folklore they have and I learned a whole bunch of interesting things about drinking games.

One teacher told us about the anxiety followed by excitement when improvising in a challenging situation paid off. In this case, a team-teaching experience did not go as expected and jolted students into greater involvement:

> We were clearly not communicating at all and the students would just watch us go back and forth and we would at times get into arguments. . . . Eventually the students actually began to work with the differences and tried to communicate what one of us was saying to the other person by trying to find the middle ground. . . . That was great. I learned so much in that class.

Finally, a professor used a multiple-theories approach to encourage students to express their views and be recognized and respected as individuals:

> When I came to this class I gave a lot of thought to it and decided to use multiple theories of social welfare—what are the philosophical underpinnings and then what types of social welfare systems might they

suggest. The reason it was important is because before, whenever I had taught that type of material, I came at it with one particular philosophical bent, which was my own. I can see in retrospect that even students who may have been sympathetic to that found it difficult because they felt they had to use that one theory. . . . The result was that this one young lady in the class said to me, "Do you really mean if I have very conservative thoughts and I am willing to be governed by those thoughts myself, that you would give me an A as well as if I were to put a very liberal concept." I said, "Of course. What I am looking for is if you thought through the implications and the program dynamics." She said, "I don't believe this, no one has ever thought about what I wanted to do. I have always just had to feed back what the teacher wanted."

Mastery of Content and Discipline at More Satisfying Levels. Some of the experiences that faculty related involve their mastery of content at a new and more satisfying level or their new connections with their own research and scholarship. In these experiences, faculty reported making a good presentation on a topic that had been difficult for them and maintaining everyone's attention. A landscape architecture professor related how he was able to maintain students' attention in relating a successful professional experience with some clients:

> Ten minutes into the class, when I sensed that everybody was looking at me. They were juniors at the time and you usually get some who are looking out the window and whatnot. I seemed to have their attention. I was walking around the room—I don't like to stand. This went on throughout the whole discussion.

A professor teaching a course in decision analysis told of presenting a difficult concept related to the nature of probability on which she had lectured twenty times, and "this was the first time I did it right. . . . The lecture just went well." This was a case where the feedback that told her she was doing well came primarily from an internal judgment:

> I was getting a lot of nods but I had very little interaction, and I usually have more with it because I pause several times and ask for questions and comments. I usually get much more interaction from that lecture than I did this time. Maybe they didn't have to ask questions because I was explaining it really well. I don't know how to read that one, I don't know whether I really got across to them. It sure felt great. It was such a high coming out of there. It felt really good.

A political science professor commented on teaching new material based on his research in an improvised and spontaneous way:

I did this on the spur of the moment with no notes, and it went on for two hours into an impromptu lecture where I wasn't constrained by a podium. It was working the crowd like Donahue. I think that was probably the thing that was most stimulating about it, because when you establish close eye contact with students you get immediate feedback concerning how they are plugging in or not plugging in on various arguments.

One faculty member in chemistry said she gets exited when she "can see that they are thinking the way a chemist thinks." She went on to say,

To analyze data and try to make transparent to them how my mind works so that they can imitate me at first and then begin to do it competently themselves. Thus, they can begin to follow their problems in the same way and to bring them to a level where they are not simply regurgitating what they have been taught, but instead feel competent to arrive at conclusions themselves.

New Variations of Teaching Methods. Some of the experiences involve new variations of different teaching methods that help students to understand the course material. A professor teaching a course in cultural conflict in developing nations related how he captured students in a heightened level of interaction with the new methodology that he was developing for his research:

I followed it with an example that I have been working on in my own spare time, a new cassette tape recorder method that revolves around digitizing information and putting it onto a cassette tape so that the A side and B side can be interrelated. . . . They were also plugged into these autocassette things, so in a sense we were both experts. We could come up with a lot of interaction based on our own life situation in relationship to that technology that I was illustrating.

A professor talked about successfully teaching a complex theoretical concept that "ends up as a three-dimensional graphical model . . . to predict how many kinds of animals should live in any given place." As he recounted,

I put together a set of overheads that could overlay so that I could put this model together one piece at a time. I had tried things like that before but they didn't work. I also tried to get them involved by having the students move their seats and put their arms even farther out or less far out to communicate areas that they could dominate.

Mutual Learning: Implications for Institutions and Academic Departments

In our telephone interviews, when faculty were asked to give examples of experiences that made teaching satisfying for them, about one-third described classroom experiences. Almost two-thirds reported experiences with students that occurred after courses were completed. The majority of their reports (82 percent) were about confirming feedback from students, whereas only a few faculty (13 percent) described confirming feedback from themselves. For most of the faculty, satisfaction came from knowing about their positive effects on students. These data and the focus group stories strongly suggest that optimal teaching experiences are more often interpersonal than personal in nature. Clearly, this was the case with 28 percent of the faculty, who vividly described their social exchanges with students in class while they were teaching. The following themes emerged in the interview data as well as in the focus group dialogues.

Classroom Strategies. The research suggests that the more socially vital a classroom, the more likely it will be a place where flow experiences happen or are primed to happen. The degree of social vitality of a classroom appears to depend on the roles that the instructor and students take. On one hand, the roles of the instructor and student can be independent and noninteractive (for example, an instructor who reads his or her lecture while students do any number of things but listen); on the other hand, these roles can be highly interdependent and interactive (for example, an instructor who skillfully stages then moderates a vigorous discussion with students). In between these extremes are cases of sympathetic coaction (for example, an instructor skillfully plans a lecture and delivers it with passion, or, similarly, students give eloquent oral presentations and the instructor reverently listens). Some of the most intense flow experiences reported by faculty in this research often involved interdependent, interactive roles of instructors and students. Many faculty reported using selected students as catalysts to encourage other students to engage in the material at a heightened level of concentration and involvement.

Time on Task. Faculty identified the need for time for both the faculty member and the students to plan and prepare before the course and during the course. During the course, faculty indicated that the instructor and students share a joint responsibility. Unless students spend the time needed to understand the material in and out of class, and to complete the necessary background work for understanding the symbolic language of the discipline, they cannot create opportunities for flow experiences. Faculty said that their own planning before and during their courses was essential to maintain freshness by using new ideas and research in the field. They also said that some element of doubt or anxiety in their ability to succeed helped them to be more fresh and creative in their approach. Csikszentmihalyi's (1990) indication that to attain flow there must be high challenge that slightly outpaces current skills may describe this need.

Need for Goals and Feedback. The research reviewed by Csikszentmihalyi (1988, 1990) suggests that both the instructor and the students have to have meaningful and somewhat compatible goals. These goals have to be clear and unambiguous and feedback about the accomplishment of the goals has to be continually available. Natural channels of feedback have to be opened up through the encouragement of spontaneity and a more favorable balance between formative feedback, such as constructive comments, and evaluative feedback, such as the grading of performances. The performances of instructors and students have to be coordinated. A classroom team of students and the instructor, capable of accomplishing more as a unit than as a loose collection of individuals, has to be formed.

Opportunities to Talk About Teaching. Faculty said that there are abundant opportunities for intrinsic rewards in teaching, but that they need reminders of these rewards from peers and feedback from students. Discussions about teaching in faculty meetings and other forums can help by providing faculty with opportunities to talk about their goals and to share ideas with one another. Dissemination of teaching products, such as syllabi, videotapes, and portfolios, helps in that teaching can be externalized for observation and discussion outside of the classroom.

Flexible Teaching Assignments. Flexibility in teaching assignments also helps to increase the intrinsic rewards. Only some faculty can attain flow in large lectures. New faculty need opportunities to become oriented to new courses by not having total responsibility for them. Opportunities for small classes help, since faculty can more easily engage students and communicate with them. Opportunities for immediate feedback help, whether through small group or recitation discussions soon after large lectures, through meetings with students in faculty offices, or through work with students in independent study. Opportunities to teach students who are majors and, it is hoped, more committed to the discipline helps in that faculty may continually engage in the learning process with students. Opportunities to bring their research into their teaching helps, but at a less specialized level, at a level of abstraction that students can understand by finding parallels to known material and by becoming familiar with research methods and processes.

Administrator Involvement. Both the theory on intrinsic rewards and the analysis of the memorable teaching experiences suggest actions that institutional administrators can take to support opportunities for intrinsic rewards. Administrators can work with their faculty to understand their teaching skills and goals and to match them with challenging, but not overwhelming, teaching assignments. They can help faculty find the time to concentrate on teaching by working with them to balance their teaching demands with their other challenges in an efficient way. They can help faculty plan for their teaching, not just to find time to develop materials but to find time to interact with colleagues and students in an effort to test out ways to convey these materials in meaningful ways.

Implications for Disciplines and Professions

In recounting their memorable experiences, the faculty in our study communicated a sense of how they see their disciplines in relationship to teaching.

Defining Pedagogy Within Each Discipline. For many faculty, the goal in teaching was to present an understanding of the underpinning of thought and histories of their disciplines, to present how different models and different levels of sophistication in understanding the disciplines have evolved. In this way, they encouraged students to see multiple points of view and different perspectives and to understand that there are no correct answers. They wanted students to learn how to think like professionals in the disciplines, an endeavor in which there are often no right answers. They wanted to move students away from a dependence on the teacher as presenter of facts to a sense of competence with the material. They wanted students to learn how they as professionals think, analyze, and learn within their disciplines. Many professors said that they get most excited about the classes for which they have to prepare new material that they are learning, so that they can demonstrate how they learn. Some said that they like to redo their courses every year. These themes are similar to Shulman's (1989) definition of a pedagogy of substance, where he argues that teaching methods cannot be separated from the content. Professional associations can help in this area by sponsoring presentations and written material that address the task of teaching difficult but critical concepts in their respective fields.

Conditions for Mutual Flow May Depend on Discipline. In reviewing these experiences, it becomes evident that some disciplines or content areas may provide more opportunities for mutual flow experiences than do others. For example, it may be more difficult to have a mutual flow experience while teaching mathematics than while teaching ethics. Content may need to be redefined to allow more spontaneous exchanges between instructors and learners. Csikszentmihalyi (personal communication, December 1992) suggests the salience of disciplinary differences when he cites interviews with Nobel Prize winners in the natural sciences, social sciences, and humanities and the arts on how, as an example, they view honesty. For mathematicians, honesty is respect for the laws of nature. For economists, honesty is trust by one's peers; if people doubt the word of an economist or think that data were fudged, the economist's career may be finished. For humanities and the arts, honesty is adherence to one's true feelings and visions. The reference point moves from an external position in mathematics to an interactive position in economics, to an internal position in the arts. It would seem that the less interactive the reference point used by a faculty member in conveying his or her discipline, the more difficult it may be to produce conditions that facilitate mutual flow. The ways in which mutual flow is experienced in the disciplines remain to be investigated. Research sponsored by the professional associations is warranted.

References

Csikszentmihalyi, M. "The Flow Experience and Its Significance for Human Psychology." In M. Csikszentmihalyi and I. S. Csikszentmihalyi (eds.). *Optimal Experience: Psychological Studies of Flow in Consciousness.* Cambridge, England: Cambridge University Press, 1988.

Csikszentmihalyi, M. *Flow: The Psychology of Optimal Experience.* New York: HarperCollins, 1990.

Menges, R. J. "Maintaining Motivation for Teaching." Paper presented at the American Association of Higher Education Forum on Faculty Roles and Rewards, San Antonio, Texas, January 1993.

Shulman, L. "Toward a Pedagogy of Substance." *AAHE Bulletin,* 1989, *41* (10), 8–13.

ROBERT C. FROH is associate director of evaluation and research at the Center for Instructional Development, Syracuse University.

ROBERT J. MENGES is professor of education and social policy at Northwestern University, Evanston, Illinois, and senior researcher for the National Center on Post-Secondary Teaching, Learning, and Assessment.

CHARLES J. WALKER is professor of psychology at St. Bonaventure University, St. Bonaventure, New York.

*The professional portfolio can move faculty work from the private to
the public arena, providing a rich representation of faculty work.*

Representing Faculty Work:
The Professional Portfolio

Robert C. Froh, Peter J. Gray, Leo M. Lambert

The purpose of this chapter is to provide guidance to faculty and university
administrators in their efforts to document how faculty spend their time
and to make judgments regarding the distribution of resources and other
elements of the faculty reward system. In order to accomplish these two
tasks, a number of issues need to be addressed: What constitutes faculty
work, that is, what is the range of legitimate activities for faculty? What is
the relative importance of the various activities and hence their weight or
influence in the distribution of rewards? What are the criteria for judging
various levels of quality and quantity of these activities? What is acceptable
evidence of quality and quantity relative to the various activities? What are
appropriate, effective, and efficient ways to collect, analyze, and report
evidence? These questions must be addressed in a way that is sensitive to
the priorities of the academic unit, the assignment of the individual faculty
member, and the characteristics of the discipline involved.

Legitimate Faculty Work

The consensus on what constitutes legitimate faculty work has changed
over the last 125 years. From the time when Harvard College was established in 1636 until the 1800s, there was nearly universal agreement that
"the prime business of American professors . . . must be regular and
assiduous class teaching" (1869, Charles W. Eliot, president, Harvard
College; Boyer, 1990, p. 4). However, with the establishment of the land
grant institutions as a result of the Morrill Act of 1862, the goal of providing
service to society, with the ultimate purpose of transforming the United

States from an agricultural to an industrial society, was added to the definition of legitimate faculty work. Around the turn of the century, when educators were greatly influenced by the German research universities, the notion of scholarly research began to be included as a component of faculty work and, in some cases, even attained supremacy. "Each appointee [was required] to sign an agreement that his promotion in rank and salary would depend chiefly upon his research productivity" (1895, William Rainey Harper, president, University of Chicago; Boyer, 1990, p. 9). However, as Boyer (1990, pp. 9–10) observed, throughout most of American higher education the emphasis on research and graduate education remained the exception rather than the rule; the principal mission at most of the nation's colleges and universities continued to be education of undergraduates. And the land grant colleges, especially, took pride in service.

It was not until after World War II that, on a widespread basis, research became an integral part of faculty work. This shift occurred because of the great influx into the national universities of faculty with Ph.D.'s who "sought to replicate the research climate that they themselves had recently experienced" (Boyer, 1990, p. 10). In this new climate, discipline-based departments became the foundation of faculty allegiance, and being a scholar was now virtually synonymous with being an academic professional.

The process occurred in two stages. The World War II veterans who took advantage of the GI Bill received their undergraduate education in institutions with faculty who believed that teaching was the primary component of faculty work. They then went on to do graduate work, to earn Ph.D.'s, and to be hired in record numbers by colleges and universities to teach the baby-boom generation as undergraduates. Because of their own experience as undergraduates and the roles that they were hired to play, those educated just after World War II retained a respect for undergraduate teaching and, if they were at land grant institutions, for service as well. It was not until a generation later, when post–World War II baby boomers swelled the enrollment of Ph.D. programs and were hired by colleges and universities for their research talents and not their commitment to teaching, that research began to overwhelm teaching and service.

There were at least two reasons for this shift in emphasis. In the late 1960s and 1970s, there was a rise in the availability of research funds from the federal government and a gradual decrease in the number of undergraduate enrollments. The first factor motivated institutions and faculty to put themselves in a strong position to compete for funds by developing research-oriented programs that focused much of their teaching energy on graduate students. The second factor resulted in keen competition for faculty positions; consequently, research credentials became increasingly salient components of young faculty members' résumés. The commitment to undergraduate teaching, in turn, became less important: "At many of the nation's four-year institutions, the focus had moved from the student to the professoriate. . . . The problem was that the research mission, which was appropriate for some institutions, created a shadow over the entire higher learning enterprise. . . . At the same time that American higher education was expanding in terms of the number and range of students enrolled, the standards used to measure academic prestige continued to be narrowed. Increasingly, professors were expected to conduct research and publish results." (Boyer, 1990, pp. 12–13).

This trend continued through the 1980s and into the 1990s. However, the further decline in undergraduate enrollments has made for even stiffer competition for faculty positions. This has meant that institutions in a position to hire new faculty are able to demand strong research records and subsequent research productivity. This is the case even in traditionally teaching-oriented liberal arts and four-year comprehensive colleges where research activities have not been required for promotion and tenure.

These changes have inevitably caused tensions within institutions among faculty who came to them at different times. And, as numerous national reports, scholarly studies, and articles in the popular media indicate, there are major tensions between faculty and undergraduate students, their parents, and others who view quite differently the relative importance of the various components of faculty work.

As a result of these tensions, there now seems to be a growing expectation among the public, professors, and academic administrators that, first, as members of the professoriate, faculty must devote a reasonable amount of time and effort to all three areas (teaching, service, and research) and, second, the faculty reward system must be sensitive to all three areas by appropriately recognizing various levels of competence and achievement.

It is important to stress that each discipline defines the professional work of faculty in its own terms and from its own perspective. Thus, a key challenge to an evolving reward system is to develop ways to communicate these discipline-specific factors to those in other fields.

In order to be able to document how faculty spend their time so that this information can be used to make judgments regarding the distribution of resources and other elements of the faculty reward system, there must be clear operational definitions of teaching, research, and service. In this way the first question posed at the beginning of this chapter—What constitutes faculty work, or what is the range of legitimate activities for faculty?—can be answered.

Traditional Definitions of Faculty Work

In this section, the three central components of faculty work are described in more specific terms.

Teaching. The quantitative definition of teaching as faculty work typically focuses on course load, that is, the number of credit hours assigned to a faculty member, including both undergraduate and graduate classes as well as related activities such as advising and field supervision. It is appropriate to ask to what extent the following count as teaching activities: noncredit teaching, curriculum and course improvement and development, class preparation, tutoring or one-on-one work with students, student assessment and evaluation, lower-division service courses, research, writing, and consulting in areas related to teaching, and other ways in which student learning is facilitated.

The qualitative definition of teaching concerns personal characteristics and behaviors that a faculty member is expected to exhibit in relation to teaching and related activities. These often include being well organized, communicating clearly, being flexible, having high expectations of students, treating students with respect, returning assignments in a timely manner, grading fairly, and promoting appropriate student outcomes with respect to their learning and development.

The task of deciding what activities constitute the domain of teaching and how to evaluate them is not easy. The same is true for service.

Service. Service can take place within many different spheres. There is institutional service (for example, committee work), disciplinary service (for example, professional association work), professional or community service (for example, application of academic expertise outside the institution, not as part of teaching or research, such as editing a journal or consulting), and private service (for example, volunteer nonacademic work with local, regional, national, or international organizations) (see Smock, 1992).

As is the case with teaching, enumeration of service-related activities can be a fairly straightforward process of logging the number of hours spent. However, evaluation of these accomplishments is even more difficult than determination of the impact of teaching on student learning and development because of the extensive and complicated set of variables that influence the effectiveness of service activities.

Research. What is often called scholarly work is generally defined by its product, not its purpose or process (Smock, 1992). The purpose and general process of research may include the advancement of knowledge, the creation of new knowledge, the integration of knowledge, and the application of knowledge. Assessment of the quantity and quality of research at this level is often not part of faculty review. Instead, faculty are judged in terms of the quantity and quality of research products. These products can include books, chapters, monographs, refereed journal articles, conference papers, review essays or book reviews, textbooks, encyclopedia entries, funded research project proposals and final reports, exhibitions or collections (creation of works of art or architecture), performances or the directing of performances of works of art, and published proceedings of scholarly or professional presentations.

At the beginning of any discussion about faculty work, it is critical that those involved, including faculty, administrators, and students, reach reasonable consensus about what constitutes the activities and outcomes of teaching, service, and research. For many fields, this three-part structure has remained primarily intact; for others, new structures, often based on Boyer's (1990) and Rice's (1991) approach, have been found more appropriate.

Using Portfolios to Represent Scholarly Work Within the Disciplines

Up to this point, the use of portfolios has been almost exclusively limited to the representation of teaching activities. Extension of the use of portfolios to represent all faculty work will require acceptance at the academic department level since the department represents the intersection of campus, disciplinary, and professional communities. In order to make professional portfolios acceptable, practices currently used to ensure quality scholarship, such as self-study and peer review, must be adapted to assess the merit of portfolios.

Teaching portfolios are a good tool for meeting the local need to demonstrate teaching quality. But a broader focus in the development of professional portfolios can help faculty at all stages of their careers demonstrate, in one dossier, the balance and quality of their skills in teaching, research, and service. The challenge is to find ways in which to appropriately represent teaching, research, and service in a single portfolio. The most common current practice is to require readers of a faculty portfolio to weigh a curriculum vitae against a teaching portfolio or some other evidence of teaching quality, and to draw conclusions regarding the faculty member's balance in scholarship and the relative importance placed on teaching, research, and service.

Using Portfolios to Form a Bridge Between the Campus Community and the Disciplinary Community. To make the professional portfolio an accepted vehicle for representing all of the professional work of faculty, it must meet the demands of both the campus community and the disciplinary community. Some possibilities for accomplishing this task are as follows: (1) Work with the disciplinary and professional associations to establish guidelines that encourage or require the use of portfolios in the recruitment for all faculty positions. (2) Work with public and private research funding sources to require a broader representation of the professional work of the principal investigators within funding proposals. This requirement might include a demonstration of their accomplishments across various activities in the areas of research, teaching, and community service. It might also include some reflective statements on how the current research fits within a broader research agenda and within their overall professional development. This approach could be used to encourage and judge more holistic approaches to research. (3) When research or other scholarly writing is submitted for review, require a statement about the work's relationship to the author's professional development. (4) When department or program reviews are conducted, require each faculty member to submit a portfolio that contains a statement about how his or her personal goals correspond to department or program goals.

Representing Professional Activities Within the Disciplines. To make professional portfolios valued within the disciplines and professions, a variety of professional activities must be valued. Under the auspices of a project at Syracuse, a number of professional associations have proposed broader definitions of scholarly or professional work that might be represented in portfolios (see Adam and Roberts, this volume). The American Historical Association proposes a variety of scholarly activities following the Rice (1991) and Boyer (1990) formulation of scholarship (advancement, integration, application, and transformation of knowledge). The American Assembly of Collegiate Schools of Business proposes scholarly activities within the areas of basic scholarship (creation of new knowledge), applied scholarship (application, transfer, and interpretation of knowledge in relation to management practice and teaching), and instructional development (enhancement of the educational value of instructional efforts in institutions and in the discipline). A consortium of associations representing faculty in the arts proposes that creative work and research activities in theater include areas of creating theater, studying theater and its influences, advancing the pedagogy of theater, and applying theater and facilitating theater activities. The American Chemical Society proposes scholarship areas of research, application, teaching, and outreach. These disciplines or professions represent professional work in different ways with different definitions, different levels of detail, and different values as to the relative importance of various activities. These cross-disciplinary differences in part explain why it is essential to consider the values of the disciplinary community carefully in the development of a professional portfolio.

Requirements for Portfolios to Represent Scholarship More Broadly. The foundation of a professional portfolio is the reflective statement that integrates what faculty value with the values of the community. To support this integration, academic departments must clearly state their own needs and goals. They then must encourage faculty members to articulate what they value, to indicate how those values respond to department needs and goals, and to provide samples of products from work that has meaning both to the individual faculty member and to the department.

Several recent efforts from the teaching portfolio area suggest ways to use portfolios to represent broader facets of faculty work. Seldin (1991) demonstrated ways in which to incorporate teaching goals and philosophy within the context of activities throughout one's career. He attempted to show how quality can be represented through inclusion of such information as the results of teaching evaluations. Edgerton, Hutchings, and Quinlan (1991) showed how the matching of selected artifacts of scholarship in teaching with reflections on those artifacts can demonstrate what is important to faculty. Shulman (1989), in research conducted primarily at secondary schools, suggested the need for a subject matter pedagogy where faculty teach in a way that shows how they relate to their respective disciplines and how they can get students to do the same. The Syracuse project on defining scholarship in the disciplines suggests that scholarly activity is valued and recognized in unique ways within each discipline. And research on intrinsic rewards suggests that when faculty recall memorable teaching events, these events often revolve around the discovery of ways to convey to students the basic principles and methodologies that the faculty find intrinsically rewarding in their disciplines. They also find that engendering these intrinsic rewards among their students is satisfying (see Froh, Menges, and Walker, this volume).

What is needed to extend the work on teaching portfolios to professional portfolios is a reflective essay that represents the faculty member's thinking in all major areas of faculty work. Ideally, this essay is supported by artifacts that represent how the faculty member has assessed his or her own professional development and thus closely approximates documentation of the answer to the question, "Which two or three experiences are most memorable to you in your development as a professional in your discipline?" The answer to this question may produce a variety of reflections on activities such as writing a specific article, making a presentation, or interacting with a significant mentor or students.

The objective is to present the case or story that best represents the type of work that faculty value most. The representation could include activities that show how the professional work has evolved. The selection and reflection of events should represent moments in teaching, research or creative efforts, and service. The point is to create opportunities for faculty to represent their deeper identities as professionals.

The challenge is to use portfolios to demonstrate quality in faculty work in new ways. For example, the standard approach to judging the quality of research is to count publications in refereed and nonrefereed journals. But this approach does not incorporate sufficient faculty judgment about the quality of the research and how the samples might represent a significant step forward in the research or creative effort of the author. When colleagues are asked to judge the quality of teaching, the standard approach is to ask them to visit a class and write a summary of what they saw. But a review of videotapes of selected instructional sequences may be a more appropriate representation of teaching. In writing, faculty are never judged by their first drafts. But for whatever reason, in the classroom, judgments based on first appearances are regarded as appropriate.

Faculty in some fields may find it useful to document the process of their scholarly or creative work and to describe the rationales that guided their decision making. This kind of documentation can be vital since a professional portfolio may be read by faculty from other disciplines who have had little experience with the relevant field and lack a working knowledge of its terminology and processes.

The push for professional portfolios comes at a time when new ways for ensuring quality research are in demand. Portfolios could represent both self-reflection and peer review. For teaching, a peer review might include a written review of videotapes of classes prepared by the instructor in an attempt to show how she or he helps students grasp particularly difficult concepts in the discipline. For research, a peer review might focus on how a sequence of publications demonstrates the author's movement in a creative direction.

Suggested Criteria for Reviewing Portfolios. To encourage the adoption of professional portfolios, faculty must have an opportunity not only to review these products within their disciplines and to comment on the quality of professional work represented, but also to generate ideas on how best to represent certain types of work such as teaching. Lynton (1993) has suggested criteria for reviewing faculty work represented within professional portfolios: (1) The work is reasoned and reflective; the presentation demonstrates expertise in making choices in a given context, responsiveness to unanticipated developments, and creativity in developing a scholarly approach; (2) the work results in new knowledge from a specific situation and demonstrates its validity and significance; and (3) the work involves communication of new knowledge to others. The phrase "new knowledge" might be modified to "new and fresh variations of the content." These criteria constitute a starting point for judgments of portfolio quality in self-study and peer review situations.

Principles of Professional Portfolio Development

Having introduced definitions of teaching, research, and service and provided an overview of the use of the professional portfolio in higher education, we offer the following discussion, incorporating eight general principles of portfolio development, as a chapter summary.

PRINCIPLE 1: *The professional portfolio has utility at every stage of an academic career.*

Professional portfolios are used today by a wide range of scholars, from graduate students who are just beginning doctoral programs to senior, tenured faculty members. Ideally, portfolio development is not a "one-shot" activity but rather a cumulative, reflective process that extends throughout one's professional career. As summarized in Table 6.1, the professional portfolio can be viewed as basic and integral to advancement to the next stage of one's academic career. At each stage, portfolio development can help scholars reflect on past accomplishments and activities, chart future professional goals, and provide selective documentation to decision makers (promotion and tenure committees, hiring committees, and so on).

Reflecting on Past Accomplishments and Achievements. Well-administered graduate programs conduct annual reviews of graduate students to inform assistantship reappointment decisions and to ensure that students are making satisfactory academic progress. This is an ideal point to begin encouraging aspiring academics to prepare professional portfolios; this practice both serves an obvious developmental purpose for graduate students and substantially improves decision making for the academic department. For graduate students nearing the end of their doctoral programs, a "stock taking" of teaching, research, and service accomplishments via the professional portfolio is also invaluable preparation for the academic job hunt.

At many institutions, faculty at all levels of seniority are required to submit annual updates of their curricula vitae to the dean. Too often, this is a rote activity in which recent publications and presentations are added, lists of courses taught are adjusted, and memberships on departmental or

Table 6.1. Use of Portfolios by Scholars at Varying Levels of the Academic Career Ladder

Level	Purpose of Portfolio
Early graduate school	Stimulate the collection of scholarly artifacts pertaining to teaching and research
	Promote reflection about initial teaching and other professional experiences
	Encourage discussion about professional activities with faculty mentors
Late graduate school	Stimulate thinking about a philosophy of teaching and a future research agenda
	Assist in the academic job hunt
Pretenure years	Facilitate promotion review
	Facilitate tenure review
	Encourage discussion about professional growth with colleagues, department chairs, and deans
Posttenure years	Encourage reflection about professional growth throughout one's academic career

institutional committees are updated. In contrast, updating of a portfolio may require significantly more reflection (and work). Faculty who update their portfolios may wish to ask such questions as, "Did my student evaluations improve to reflect my efforts to enhance classroom discussions?" "What progress have I achieved on my research agenda?" "Have my contributions to departmental governance improved policies and practice?" Inherent to these questions is the comparison of *outcomes* to *desired goals*.

Charting Future Professional Goals. Graduate students about to embark on academic careers require substantive guidance about their future professional directions. Questions that graduate students may discuss with mentors as an important part of professional portfolio construction include the following: "What type of institution would be the best fit for me for my first professional job?" "What are promising directions for my future research?" "Which aspects of my teaching need special attention during my first semester of professional employment?"

For faculty, examination of professional accomplishments may lead to renewed emphases or new directions in their academic lives. For example, a faculty member who has just completed a new book or brought a major research grant to successful completion may decide to take up the challenge of redesigning his or her undergraduate course and experimenting with new teaching methods. Ideally, these decisions are made carefully and reflexively in consultation with valued colleagues and key administrators such as department chairs.

Providing Selective Documentation to Decision Makers. The key word here is *selective*. A major challenge in professional portfolio construction is to decide "how much is enough" when the portfolio will be used for personnel decision making (such as hiring, promotion, or tenure). Too much data in the professional portfolio can be unwieldy and, worse, misleading by creating the impression of a candidate who is not discriminating or who is attempting to "snow" the committee with paper. In contrast, too sparse a portfolio may convey a lack of substance and professional experience. The essence of good professional portfolio construction is to convey as much depth and richness as possible by providing selective evidence of professional accomplishments.

PRINCIPLE 2: *Before any thought is given to professional portfolio construction, scholars should clearly understand what their institutions expect of them in terms of professional work and what evidence of successful performance is deemed appropriate.*

Especially in informing personnel decisions, the professional portfolio is an ideal means of representing faculty work. But portfolio construction should follow, not precede, substantive discussions about the relative weight that teaching, research, and service will be given in the personnel decision at hand. In turn, the portfolio contents should at least roughly reflect the relative weight assigned to each professional activity; the nature of the evidence collected for each professional activity should also be discussed in advance to ensure its acceptability to decision makers.

The exercise of constructing a professional portfolio can be hollow and disappointing if the questions of appropriate balance of professional activities and acceptable evidence of accomplishments are ignored. For promotion and tenure decisions especially, faculty members are in jeopardy if they fail to understand the expectations of their faculty colleagues, chairs, and deans and what evidence of accomplishments is deemed appropriate by these parties.

PRINCIPLE 3: *The format and contents of the portfolio should be adjusted to suit particular purposes, audiences, and local norms.*

As noted above, professional portfolios may be constructed for a variety of reasons. For maximum effectiveness, scholars may need to develop different versions of their portfolios for different contexts. They should consider the following questions: (1) Is the portfolio being developed for *formative* (professional growth and planning) or *summative* purposes (promotion or tenure review or a job application)? (2) Who are the key audiences for the portfolio? (3) How much material is appropriately included in the portfolio? (How much can readers be reasonably expected to review?)

Increasingly in higher education, professional portfolios are being requested of prospective faculty by search committees. Applicants may choose to develop summaries or brief dossiers highlighting key aspects of the portfolios and submit them with their curricula vitae in the initial stages of the application process. In the later stages of the search, committees may wish to examine more expansive, detailed portfolios for all finalists invited to campus. In both cases, applicants may wish to tailor their portfolios to demonstrate a "fit" with the position sought, for example, one version emphasizing a balance of teaching, research, and service activities for a position at a land grant university, and a second version emphasizing graduate teaching and research accomplishments for a position at a doctorate-granting university.

In developing a portfolio for personal development and planning purposes, a comprehensive professional portfolio may be desirable. Scholars should carefully review potential portfolio artifacts, discuss professional goals and aspirations with colleagues and administrators, and write thoughtful reflective statements. Again, institutional expectations are of prime importance even in the case of a portfolio designed for developmental (formative) purposes: The balance of teaching, research, and service expected of faculty at a given institution still must be considered.

If faculty from various departments and disciplines are serving on committees making summative decisions, especially promotion and tenure decisions, an effort must be made to communicate to them the priorities of the candidate's department, assignments typically given to the faculty member, and the range of scholarly activities considered appropriate in the faculty member's discipline. Statements presently being developed by a number of professional and academic societies may assist in this process. Further, it is essential to describe the criteria for quality performance in the faculty member's discipline in an introductory statement in the professional portfolio and to include supporting documentation.

PRINCIPLE 4: *The process of portfolio development is as important as, if not more important than, the final product (the portfolio).*

In developing portfolios for either formative or summative purposes, faculty consistently remark that the process of developing a portfolio is both challenging and worthwhile. Portfolio construction demands serious contemplation of and reflection on important questions: "What are my strengths as a teacher?" "What is my best evidence of teaching effectiveness?" "What is my philosophy of teaching?" "What are my most significant contributions to scholarship?" "What are my most important service contributions to my institution?" In grappling with these questions and taking stock of their accomplishments, faculty may discover new insights about their professional lives.

Development of professional portfolios also presents a wonderful opportunity for faculty (and graduate students at the beginning of their academic careers) to discuss their scholarly accomplishments with colleagues or mentors. Occasions for reflection and discussion about teaching, research, and service with a colleague or mentor are rare in higher education, but portfolio preparation provides a natural vehicle for such dialogue. Even in cases where portfolios have been developed for summative purposes, portfolio contents may set the stage for substantive discussions with key decision makers. For example, department chairs may use the portfolio review process to discuss merit pay increases and to suggest appropriate professional goals for the future.

PRINCIPLE 5: *The reflective statement is a key orienting and organizing element of the portfolio.*

Good professional portfolios are not simply compilations of "best work." In order to be maximally effective, portfolios should contain an introductory reflective essay that orients the reader to portfolio contents, reviews past accomplishments and future plans, and provides a philosophical statement about the professional and intellectual work contained in the portfolio. Writing the reflective statement is often described by faculty as one of the most difficult—but most productive—aspects of portfolio preparation.

PRINCIPLE 6: *One of the most difficult aspects of portfolio development is getting started—collecting and organizing artifacts and materials for inclusion.*

For many faculty and graduate students, the challenge of collecting far-flung materials and artifacts for inclusion in the portfolio seems daunting. Two graduate students in philosophy at Syracuse University, Greg Ganssle and David Woodruff, have metaphorically described the process of dealing with professional portfolio contents as "files and piles." In the broadest sense, the entire contents of the filing cabinets in a faculty member's office are fair game for inclusion in the professional portfolio, including collections of syllabi, examinations, student evaluations, reprints of research papers, and so on. Again, the challenge is to sort and winnow down these files into "piles" of materials and artifacts that portray an appropriate balance of professional accomplishments. To encourage graduate students to begin to collect materials early on in their academic careers, the teaching assistant program at Syracuse University provides each new arrival with an expandable, accordion file in which to collect materials for professional portfolios.

PRINCIPLE 7: *Appropriate evaluation of portfolios is a time-consuming but worthwhile effort.*

Given the care and consideration required to prepare good professional portfolios, it seems only fair that equal care and consideration be given to their review and evaluation. Portfolios do not easily lend themselves to quick, summary judgments about professional accomplishments (such as those achieved by simply counting publications on a curriculum vitae). This is, in fact, the primary virtue of portfolios—they reflect the complexity and interrelatedness of all teaching, research, and service activities.

As higher education continues to experiment with professional portfolios, more sophisticated consideration must be given to how they will be reviewed and judged, especially for promotion and tenure decisions. The time required to adequately review portfolios must be invested in the evaluation process if we are to seriously contend with the issues of measuring and valuing contributions to research, teaching, and service.

PRINCIPLE 8: *The professional portfolio must subsume the curriculum vitae in order to adequately inform important personnel decisions.*

The curriculum vitae has traditionally served as the coin of the realm in summative personnel decisions, including hiring, promotion, and tenure. But standing alone, it is an incomplete proxy for a professional portfolio, particularly with regard to providing evidence of the quality and creativity of teaching and service activities. The curriculum vitae should be included as an important element of the professional portfolio, contributing, along with the reflective essay, to a summary of accomplishments. Because the professional portfolio, and not the curriculum vitae, has the capacity to convey a true, rich picture of an academic professional life, it is incumbent on all faculty and administrators participating in personnel decisions to require carefully prepared portfolios as the new standard for documentation of professional accomplishments.

Professional portfolios can become a tool for faculty to proclaim their own goals, and their understanding of department, campus, and community goals, and to show what they are doing to integrate those goals. Portfolios can include products that represent changes in what faculty have been doing. Portfolios can represent work in the discipline or profession for judgments of quality at the level of the individual faculty member, but they can also be used to convey new ideas. In essence, professional portfolios can move faculty work from the private to the public arena.

References

Boyer, E. L. *Scholarship Reconsidered: Priorities for the Professoriate.* Princeton, N.J.: Carnegie Foundation for the Advancement of Teaching, 1990.

Edgerton, R., Hutchings, P., and Quinlan, K. *The Teaching Portfolio: Capturing the Scholarship in Teaching.* Washington, D.C.: American Association of Higher Education, 1991.

Lynton, E. "The Scholarly Function: Common Characteristics and Criteria." Paper presented at the AAHE Forum on Faculty Roles and Rewards, San Antonio, Texas, January 1993.

Rice, R. E. "The New American Scholar: Scholarship and the Purposes of the University." *Metropolitan Universities Journal,* 1991, *1* (4), 7–18.

Seldin, P. *The Teaching Portfolio.* Boston: Anker, 1991.

Shulman, L. "Toward a Pedagogy of Substance." *AAHE Bulletin,* 1989, *41* (10), 8–13.

Smock, S. "Evaluating Non-Traditional Forms of Scholarship." Paper presented at the conference Scholarship Reconsidered: Implications for State System Universities, Harrisburg, Pennsylvania, October 1992.

ROBERT C. FROH is associate director of evaluation and research at the Center for Instructional Development, Syracuse University.

PETER J. GRAY is director of evaluation and research at the Center for Instructional Development, Syracuse University.

LEO M. LAMBERT is associate dean of the graduate school at Syracuse University.

Appendix: Departmental Statements on Faculty Rewards

Ultimately, it is at the departmental level that the quality and fairness of faculty reward systems are determined. Each department must develop its own mission statement and appropriate faculty recognition and reward plan. It is essential that the statement be inclusive and develop the sense of ownership necessary for implementation within the department. The following elements should be included in the plan:

A description of the departmental mission referencing the institutional mission and campus priorities, the nature of the discipline, and the goals of the department

The criteria on which faculty rewards will be determined and the evaluation process that will be used

Definitions, weighting systems, and structures that will be needed for implementation

Guidelines for addressing individual strengths, assignments, and changes over time in individual and departmental priorities.

Following are selected sections of statements, with minor adaptations, from two departments at Syracuse University: Economics and the Writing Program. The selections focus on the priorities and missions of the units. Each speaks to the nature of the discipline, the goals of the department, and the response of the department to the administrative charge to focus on the teaching mission and to define the range of scholarly and professional work that will be recognized within the department.

The remaining and much larger portions of the documents include detailed discussions of the evaluation process for each of the major categories of faculty work and descriptions of criteria for assessment and the weights that will be given to different activities. Limitations of space did not permit inclusion of these statements in their entirety.

The first selection, by James Follain, department chair, Department of Economics, Syracuse University, dated October 27, 1992, is as follows:

Evaluation of Research and Teaching for the Purpose of Salary Determination in the Department of Economics

Introduction. In his February 17, 1992, report to the faculty, Chancellor Shaw stated clearly his view regarding the importance of the annual review process of all faculty members. He also indicated that departments, schools, and colleges are to have well-documented plans in place to evaluate the teaching, research, advising, and service performances of all members of the faculty and that the plan to allocate salary increments must place equal emphasis on both teaching and research. Dean John Palmer affirmed these views in his spring 1992 statement to the Maxwell faculty.

This document represents the output of the review processes and our response to the calls from both Chancellor Shaw and Dean Palmer to explain our salary review process. The document contains four additional sections. The next section summarizes briefly the procedures that will be followed in the salary process.

Relative Importance of Teaching and Research. Salary increases are to be awarded to individual faculty members based upon their performance in teaching, research, advising, and service to the department, the Maxwell School, the College of Arts and Sciences, the university, and the broader community in which we work. The dominant areas of performance are teaching and research; equal emphasis is placed on both teaching and research. Advising, which includes a wide variety of activities in which faculty members interact with students outside of regular teaching assignments, is designated as a component of teaching.

Over time, the pool of funds available for salary increases within the department ought to be allocated in the following proportions: roughly speaking, 40 percent is to be allocated to teaching and advising, 40 percent is to be allocated to research, and 20 percent is allocated based upon the discretion of the chair. The chair's discretionary allotment is intended to reward unusual and extraordinary performances in research, teaching, advising, and service and to respond to various circumstances that require salary adjustments, for example, outside offers.

This 40-40-20 rule need not be adhered to strictly within each year or among all individuals. Overall performance by the faculty in research or teaching may be relatively strong in research or teaching in a particular year and, as a result, the chair may choose to deviate modestly from these proportions. Furthermore, the rule may not always be applied rigidly among all individuals each year. The chair may decide to alter the weights that apply to specific individuals in particular years who demonstrate excellent performance in one of the categories. Also, the chair may choose to alter the rule in order to encourage a person to undertake valuable activities in one of these areas, for example, develop a new course or undertake an externally sponsored research project. However, the allocation of the salary pool over several years ought to generate no less than 40 percent of the pool to research and 40 percent to teaching; furthermore, substantial deviations must be well justified to the department and the dean of the Maxwell School.

Four further remarks are aimed to clarify what follows. First, criteria for salaries are certainly connected with, but in some ways different from, criteria for promotion or tenure. Tenure, in particular, depends on issues like the quality of one's teaching, the fit between the teaching interests of the candidate and the needs of the department, the coherence of one's research program, the fit of one's research program with long-term department goals, and the pattern of output over time that may not be reflected in annual raise decisions. A separate document exists that discusses in more detail the department's criteria for tenure and promotion.

Second, the determination of evaluation criteria is a dynamic process. Each year one of the responsibilities of the Teaching and Research Evaluation Committees is to consider whether aspects of this document need revision. Furthermore, all faculty are encouraged, each fall, to express their best current thinking about criteria to the committees. A more thorough and formal review of the document is expected every three years.

Third, it is important to stress that while some aspects of the valuation problem will be expressed in terms of "weights," "discount factors," "gradients," and so on, it is *not* intended that we adopt a mechanical approach. There is no unique formula; judgments will and must be made by the committees and the department chair. All proxies are imperfect. All must be applied intelligently. All must be applied with flexibility, understanding, and sympathy.

Finally, consider a very natural question: "If I'm not going to get rewarded for _____, why should I do it?" Committee work, talking with students, proposal writing, refereeing, working on comprehensive exams, . . . where do they end up being valued? Some, like proposal writing, get rewarded in the future. Some get rewarded by the Dean's Office. Some get rewarded by good collegial relations. Some is done (refereeing?) out of a sense of personal responsibility. And some are just their own reward. Our intent is not to have a system that places a positive and unchanging weight on all activities for the purpose of salary determination. This is neither possible nor desirable. Rather, the system is intended to signal as clearly as possible the priorities of the department and to use the salary process to further those priorities. We think this system, although complex, time-consuming, and controversial, moves us in that direction.

Teaching Evaluation. An important aspect of the teaching role of the department within the thrust of the university and the college is to impart the discipline's characteristic orientation. This includes a point of view that emphasizes the interrelated nature of activities; that is, human behavior can be viewed within the context of a series of systems (for example, markets), which can be analyzed with theoretically based methods and models.

In teaching undergraduate and graduate students who major in economics, the department seeks to prepare students so that they can operate as economists in the endeavors they may pursue after they complete their study in the department. This involves teaching economics to provide students with the knowledge base, the vocabulary, the tools, and analytical habits that constitute the discipline of economics and an introduction of their application to key policy issues. Undergraduate career selection may include graduate study in economics or another discipline or initiation of a career in the public or private sector. Graduate training is more specifically directed to the production of technical economists, that is, those who apply the tools and analytical constructs of the profession in their daily work, such as college-level teaching and research. The focus and mission of service courses, those designed for nonmajors, are much the same, although the emphasis may be more on developing an understanding and appreciation of economics and the insights it can provide in a number of applied areas rather than on technical training per se. The desire of the department at all levels of instruction is to produce high-quality, broadly informed, technically able, and analytically astute students.

The teaching role also requires that teachers assist students in educational planning and career selection. To some extent all teachers advise students about learning strategies during the course of consulting about class performance, but teachers have the obligation to assist in the more formal advising activities of the university, college, and department. The desire of the department in its advising activities is to assist students in the making of class and scheduling choices appropriate to their skills, abilities, aspirations, and career choices. The expertise required to meet all these needs for the variety of students is much beyond the capabilities of most teachers. However, good advising includes recognition of student needs, knowledge of the programs and facilities to support them, and a commitment that ensures that students are appropriately served.

Research Evaluation and Salary Determination. Part of the mission of the department is the production of scholarly research that is important, intellectually deep, and that connects successfully with the research of others.

Quality of research is important. But "market" signals are important too. Peer review and recognition are the keys to both. It is, therefore, important to understand that the ranking for salary decisions is not based just on some judgment of pure intellectual quality. Work of high quality that is not published, or is published in obscure places, or published in highly regarded journals, but never cited and so never connecting with the work of others, will receive less salary reward than high-quality and widely cited work published in the top journals. In particular, we will aim for salaries that are roughly consistent with the market for academic economists. Two scholars doing work of equal quality by some intellectual measure, one in a way that the market rewards much more than the other, will have to be somewhat differentially paid to attract or retain both. Of course, we assume that faculty choose their research areas and basic methods of approach primarily on their own ideas about what is intellectually important and not in a simplistic response to salary criteria or mere market rewards.

The second selection, by Louise Wetherbee Phelps, director of the Writing Program, Syracuse University, dated December 14, 1989, and revised April 1992, is as follows:

Guidelines for Promotion and Tenure in the Writing Program

Introduction. According to its charter, "The Writing Program has responsibility for planning and implementing a comprehensive writing program for the university community. The goal of the program is to integrate writing and reading and critical thinking throughout the curriculum and to encourage continuing development of these abilities." In addition, faculty in the program have program-related and individual responsibilities for scholarship and graduate education. The Writing Program is conceived as an intellectual community that makes the university writing curriculum (undergraduate and graduate, liberal and professional) a primary site for basic and applied research, theoretical studies, graduate training, and experimentation with innovative teaching practices.

Reflecting this mission and the multidisciplinary backgrounds of its faculty, members of the Writing Program are jointly appointed to a maximum of 60 percent time in the Writing Program and 40 percent time in another department. They are diverse in their graduate training, disciplinary sources, topics and sites of research, methods, and academic affiliations. But they are unified by their scholarly interest in written language as a complex social activity and medium for intellectual development and by their commitment to education for a creative and critical literacy. Unlike many disciplines, composition and rhetoric (the central discipline for the Writing Program) integrates the search for knowledge closely with its commitments to practice in school settings and the larger world. This unusual correlation between what the faculty in the Writing Program study and what they do makes it necessary to redefine here the concepts of "scholarship," "teaching," and "service," in the usual categories of performance and achievement at the university, and to account for the ways they may overlap and merge.

Dimensions of Performance and Achievement. Candidates for tenure and promotion in the Writing Program are evaluated on two dimensions of performance and achievement that cut across the traditional categories of teaching, scholarship, and service.

Significant Intellectual Work. The university's responsibilities for teaching, scholarship, and service all reflect its commitment to increase human knowledge and make it available for personal and social use. Both its faculty and its students are participants in the processes of inquiry, discovery, critical examination, and rhetorical communication by which knowledge is created and applied.

Significant intellectual work refers to the various ways in which faculty at the university can contribute to these general goals with respect to knowledge. These include, for example, creating new knowledge or understanding; clarifying, critically examining, weighing, and revising the knowledge claims, beliefs, or understanding of others and oneself; connecting knowledge to other knowledge; preserving, restoring, and reinterpreting past knowledge; arguing knowledge claims in order to invite criticism and revision; making specialized knowledge publicly accessible and usable, especially to young learners; helping new generations to become active knowers themselves, preparing them for lifelong learning and discovery; applying knowledge in significant or innovative ways; applying esthetic, ethical, political, or spiritual values to make judgments about knowledge and its uses; and creating insight and communicating forms of experience through artistic works or performance.

The faculty of the Writing Program recognize that such significant intellectual and creative contributions may occur in any arena of faculty activity: scholarship, education, administration, professional activities and services of varied types. Often intellectual work by faculty in the Writing Program is integrated across these categories. For example, a faculty member might design and teach an experimental writing course (teaching), present its theoretical basis in a conference talk or published article (scholarship), supervise a group of instructors teaching it (administration), and act as a consultant to other universities designing or evaluating similar courses (professional activities). The quality and significant impact of the intellectual work is more important than its label. Candidates for tenure and promotion will differ legitimately in how they balance effort and achievement among these categories.

Intellectual work in a university setting may excel in various ways. Although not an exhaustive list, the following represent qualities that may distinguish respected intellectual work in any category of faculty effort: skill, care, rigor, and intellectual honesty; a "heuristic passion" for knowledge; originality; coherence, consistency, and development within a body of work; diversity of contribution; thorough knowledge and constructive use of important work by others; the habit of self-critical examination and openness to criticism and revision; sustained productivity over time; high impact and value to a local community (for example, program or college); relevance and significance to issues outside the university; effective communication and dissemination.

Depending on its scope and purpose, intellectual work of high quality may have concentrated impact on a broader front. In judging the work of its faculty, the Writing Program recognizes a wide range of possibilities for types of achievement and for the audience of intellectual work, which ranges from the esoteric, specialized, or local to the occasional breadth of a "public intellectual." The Writing Program notes particularly a distinction between the way intellectual work disseminates in scholarship and in teaching. Whereas scholarship (even when collaborative) reaches a public outside the university immediately and directly, largely through the individual's written products or creative artifacts, the impact of achievement in teaching and curriculum work is indirect and more gradual. The products of teaching (and administration as well) are students and their work, on the one hand, and a curriculum or successful program, on the other. This kind of intellectual work may be harder to demonstrate or evaluate and is appreciated and nationally recognized only over a period of time. It is nonetheless valuable to the university and the society.

Academic and Professional Citizenship. Programs, universities, and professions are from one perspective social organizations that must count on their members for energy, time, and leadership to sustain and develop them as viable, effective systems. In this sense faculty are citizens of these communities and share responsibility for their governance and advancement as communities. Faculty are evaluated for their constructive contributions to sustaining or leading the communities in which they do their professional work: program, department, or center; college; university; and disciplinary, interdisciplinary, or professional communities.

Such contributions have special significance for the Writing Program, where faculty are engaged in a joint project of program development and implementation. The program combines and integrates research and teaching functions through a collaborative social architecture within the program (faculty engage in professional development, mentoring, and cooperative projects with program teachers) and through interdisciplinary collegial connections with faculty and other units. In this respect the program operates more like a research center than a traditional department.

As in the case of intellectual work, academic and professional citizenship may be a dimension in any domain of faculty activity: for example, editing a major journal (scholarship), organizing an orientation program for new teachers (teaching), serving as a director or committee chair (administration), or serving as president of a national professional organization (professional activities and service).

The minimum requirement of academic and professional citizenship for Writing Program faculty is collegiality. Collegiality is a criterion for tenure. As defined here, collegiality includes accepting professional duties and contributing to the intellectual life and ongoing work of the Writing Program; and helping to create an environment conducive to the intellectual and professional work of others, through guidance, help, and respect for one's colleagues. Collegiality is evaluated only at the level of department or program.

In promotion decisions, achievement in academic and professional citizenship refers to effective, imaginative leadership or constructive contributions to projects or governance involving heavy responsibility and/or sustained investment of time, energy, and intellectual effort. Such achievement may equally valuably occur in the local environment (program or department, college, university), or in professional forums from regional to national to international settings.

In any review for promotion or tenure, distinguished accomplishment or promise in intellectual work carries primary weight. However, contributions as a citizen of academic and professional communities are also highly valued, especially in conjunction with intellectual work. Candidates in the Writing Program must meet more than minimum expectations in this dimension for tenure and promotion to associate professor, and distinguished contributions as an academic or professional citizen are an important consideration in weighing a candidate's eligibility for promotion to full professor.

INDEX

Accountability: of chemistry departments, 45; and teaching climate, 65
Accreditation standards: and faculty reward system, 10–11; in management and business, 32; and mission statements, 16–17
Adam, B. E., 1, 2–3, 17, 23, 61, 63
Administration: attitudes of, 7; and institutional reward structure, 5; role of, in changing faculty reward system, 13–15, 21, 77–78; support of, for intrinsic rewards, 93–94
Advisory groups, on institutional change, 75, 79–81
American Assembly of Collegiate Schools of Business (AACSB), 30–35, 61, 102
American Assembly of Collegiate Schools of Business (AACSB) Task Force on Faculty Research, 20, 31, 34–35, 61; members of, 35
American Chemical Society, 24, 102
American Chemical Society Task Force on the Definition of Scholarship in Chemistry, 45–50, 61; members of, 50
American Council of Learned Societies, 26
American Historical Association (AHA), 27–28, 61, 102
American Historical Association (AHA) Ad Hoc Committee on Redefining Scholarly Work, 7, 12, 24–30, 61; members of, 30
American Historical Association (AHA) Ad Hoc Committee on the Future of the AHA, 26, 61
Angelo, T. A., 73, 86
Anxiety, 88
Apathy, 88
Applied scholarship, 34, 54, 102. *See also* Scholarship activities; Scholarship definition
Arts disciplines: approaches to, 38; assessment techniques in, 44; authenticity in, 39; collaboration in, 40; defining work of, 35–44; definition of, 36; as disciplines, 37; equivalencies in, 43–44; evaluation issues in, 42–44; expertise in, 44; faculty responsibili-

ties in, 41–42; innovation in, 43; instruction in, 41; interrelationships of, 37–38; invention in, 39; making in, 37; perspectives for study of, 38–39; powers of, 37; priorities in, 40–41; providing opportunities in, 43; recognition vs. quality in, 43; review in, 40; simplicity and complexity in, 39–40, 42; terminology and, 36; work *about* vs. work *in*, 37, 43–44
Assessment: in arts disciplines, 44; development of programs for, 11–12; in geography discipline, 57, 58; quantity vs. quality in, 43, 70. *See also* Assessment criteria; Evaluation
Assessment criteria: context-specific, 20–21; establishment of departmental, 16, 21; institutional review and approval of, 18. *See also* Assessment
Assessment movement, 10
Association of American Geographers (AAG) Special Committee on Faculty Roles and Rewards, 50–61; members of, 61
Austin, A., 16, 22

Barrows, R., 64, 86
Basic scholarship, 33–34, 54, 102. *See also* Scholarship activities; Scholarship definition
Boredom, 88
Boyer, E. L., 6–7, 9, 12, 23, 25, 48, 51, 61, 63, 71, 73, 74, 77, 83, 86, 87, 97, 98, 99, 101, 102
Budget cutbacks: and changing priorities, 1, 67–68; and research funding, 20; and strategic planning, 84
Business disciplines. *See* Management and business disciplines

California State University, Long Beach, 82
Carnegie-Mellon University, 80
Carolinian Creed, 14
Cartwright, C. A., 83
Cavanagh, R., 75
Center for Instructional Development, 23, 26, 78

ORDERING INFORMATION

NEW DIRECTIONS FOR HIGHER EDUCATION is a series of paperback books that provides timely information and authoritative advice about major issues and administrative problems confronting every institution. Books in the series are published quarterly in spring, summer, fall, and winter and are available for purchase by subscription and individually.

SUBSCRIPTIONS for 1993 cost $45.00 for individuals (a savings of 20 percent over single-copy prices) and $60.00 for institutions, agencies, and libraries. Please do not send institutional checks for personal subscriptions. Standing orders are accepted.

SINGLE COPIES cost $14.95 when payment accompanies order. (California, New Jersey, New York, and Washington, D.C., residents please include appropriate sales tax.) Billed orders will be charged postage and handling.

DISCOUNTS for quantity orders are available. Please write to the address below for information.

ALL ORDERS must include either the name of an individual or an official purchase order number. Please submit your order as follows:
Subscriptions: specify series and year subscription is to begin
Single copies: include individual title code (such as HE1)

MAIL ALL ORDERS TO:
Jossey-Bass Publishers
350 Sansome Street
San Francisco, California 94104

FOR SINGLE-COPY SALES OUTSIDE OF THE UNITED STATES CONTACT:
Maxwell Macmillan International Publishing Group
866 Third Avenue
New York, New York 10022

FOR SUBSCRIPTION SALES OUTSIDE OF THE UNITED STATES, contact any international subscription agency or Jossey-Bass directly.

OTHER TITLES AVAILABLE IN THE
NEW DIRECTIONS FOR HIGHER EDUCATION SERIES
Martin Kramer, Editor-in-Chief